In All My Remembering

William Barnett Wade, Jr.

Parson's Porch Books

www.parsonsporchbooks.com

In All My Remembering

ISBN: Softcover 978-1-949888-41-6

Copyright © 2018 by William Barnett Wade. Jr.

All rights reserved. No part of this book may be reproduced or transmitted in any form or by any means, electronic or mechanical, including photocopying, recording, or by any information storage and retrieval system, without permission in writing from the publisher.

Photo Credit on Back Cover: Jodi Walden

In All My Remembering

Contents

Sermons Matter 9

Acknowledgments 11

Foreword 13

Introduction 17

Manger Scenes 19
   Isaiah 11:1-10; Luke 2:1-7

If I Were a Wise Man: A Wise Man's Story 24
   Psalm 72:1-10; Matthew 2:1-12

Who's Whispering in Your Ear? 29
   Exodus 2:1-15; Hebrews 11:23-28

Highs and Lows 35
   2 Corinthians 4:3-6; Mark 9:2-9

No Plausible Words of Wisdom 39
   2 Corinthians 2:1-5

Palm Sunday Rocks 44
   Luke 19:28-44

Maundy Thursday 49
   John 13:1-17, 34-35

Good Friday 53
   John 18:28-40

The Last Laugh 58
   John 20:1-18

Gone Fishing 63
   John 21:1-19

A New Community 67
  Acts 2
All Dogs Go to Heaven? 72
  Genesis 7:1-5; 9:8-13; Romans 8:18-24
From Childhood 79
  2 Timothy 3:14-15
In Lieu of Advice 84
  Luke 15:1-3a; 11-32
Remembered 88
  Deuteronomy 26:1-11
Freedom 93
  Exodus 6:1-13; Luke 4:16-21
Bearing and Following the Word into the World 100
  Luke 10:25-28; Romans 12:9-21
Troubled Waters 107
  Mark 4:35-41
Holy Ground 113
  Exodus 3:1-6
Sighs Too Deep for Words 117
  Psalms 46; Romans 8:18-39
Why Church? 122
  John 15:4-5; Ephesians 1:15-23
Go Figure 127
  1 Timothy 6:6-8, 17-19; 2 Corinthians 8:1-15
Patriotism 132
  Matthew 5:14-16; Philippians 3:17-21

What Holds Us Together 138
    Romans 12: 9-21
Foolishness 143
    1 Corinthians 1:18-31
Blessed 149
    Genesis 1-2:3
In All My Remembering 155
    Philippians 1:1-11

Sermons Matter

Parson's Porch Books is delighted to present to you this series called *Sermons Matter*.

We believe that many of the best writers are pastors who take the role of preacher seriously. Week in, and week out, they exegete scripture, research material, write and deliver sermons in the context of the life of their congregation in their given community.

We further believe that sermons are extensions of Holy Scripture which need to be published beyond the manuscripts which are written for delivery each Sunday. Books serve as a vehicle for the sermon to continue to proclaim the Good News of the Morning to a broader audience.

William Barnett Wade, Jr. is a seasoned pastor who takes his preaching seriously. This collection of sermons will teach other preachers what a good sermon is, and it will help others in their Christian faith.

We celebrate the wonderful occasion of the preaching event in Christian worship when the Pastor speaks, the People listen and the Work of the Church proceeds.

Take, Read, and Heed.

David Russell Tullock, M.Div., D.Min.
Publisher
Parson's Porch Books

Acknowledgments

I am grateful to the people of the First Presbyterian Church of Covington, Georgia and to others in the Covington community who have listened and responded to my sermons over the last 32 years. I give thanks for those who have encouraged me and challenged me as we have shared a partnership in witnessing to the Gospel of Jesus Christ and God's love for the world. I am grateful to my family, neighbors and friends who have inspired my preaching, some who have shown up in these sermons as examples of faithfulness, love and kindness. I am thankful for my wife, Theodosia, who has taught me much about how to live in faith, hope and love. She has spent many hours, not only listening from the pew, but reading and reflecting on these sermons and helping to collect and edit them for this publication. I am grateful to my colleague, Dan Walden, along with Peni Kehoe, who have provided valuable assistance in putting together this project, and to Jodi Walden for her photography. Thank you also to David Russell Tullock and Parson's Porch Books for the good work they do, for asking me to engage in this project, and for editing and publishing it.

Audio versions of many of these and other sermons preached at First Presbyterian Church Covington, Georgia are available at www.fpccov.org.

Foreword

According to an old preachers' tale, a parishioner asks her pastor, "How long did it take to prepare that sermon you preached this morning?" "All my life," replies the preacher. "All my life."

William Wade's remarkable collection of sermons demonstrates the truth behind that old story. His entire life – long, faithful, observant, filled with compassion; a life spent placing one foot in front of the other, in season and out, in obedience to his call – is poured into these sermons, and they are rich with the aroma of wisdom's costly perfume poured out for others.

I have spent over four decades teaching preaching to seminarians (indeed, Billy Wade was one of my students years ago). On the surface, the formula for a good sermon is simple. Like a recipe from the Fanny Farmer cookbook, you take a cup of biblical interpretation, two measures of theology, a handful of contemporary references, a pinch of drama and suspense, and there you are. But experienced preachers know that superb cuisine in the pulpit defies formulas and demands more than a list of basic ingredients thrown together. Like a great and loving cook, William Wade knows how long to let ideas simmer, how to whisk together the great themes from the scripture with the satisfactions and vexations of everyday life, and how to improvise. He reaches for a biblical commentary on his bookshelf, only to find, tucked between the volumes, an old postcard with a Rembrandt painting of an angel whispering to St. Matthew. The commentary finds its way into the sermon, but so does the postcard. He can sit for a while in a cemetery and realize that "cemeteries are not always quiet places. If you listen, you can hear the stories." Those stories are stirred into the proclamation, and they make a savory dish.

On his CNN news program, the journalist Wolf Blitzer was once interviewing a spokesperson for the White House. Blitzer would ask question after question about White House policy, but the spokesperson deflected each question in favor of an increasingly histrionic defense of the president. The longer the interview went on, the more impassioned the spokesperson became, until, at one point, Blitzer interjected, "Calm down a minute, we don't have to yell." Even when William Wade is at his most passionate, it is noteworthy how calm his voice is. Even in the written versions of these sermons, one can perceive that he does not shout, reminiscent of what Isaiah says of God's servant: "He will not cry or lift up his voice or make it heard in the street" (Is 42:2).

Given the calm and even cadences of these sermons, we might overlook how prophetic they actually are. In William Wade's theological world, the gospel comes to comfort, nurture, and sustain, but it also comes to call us out of our self-absorption and to shake the foundations of our assumed realities. These sermons often stir the waters, not because Wade enjoys being a troublemaker, but because he strives to follow his Lord. "Sometimes," he says, "I wish Jesus would just be quiet. But I've committed my life to trusting him, and sometimes I follow through."

If we had to single out one quality of these sermons that shines brightest, we would be hard-pressed. But certainly, high on the list would be their deep participation in the truth of the incarnation. These sermons are never abstract but infused throughout with the conviction that God has dwelled among us in Christ, and, because of that, the places, and people, and objects around us matter eternally. Wade sees God present and at work in backyard neighbors, church suppers and family meals, children at play, exchanges in barbeque restaurants, and through the pains and memories in nursing homes. "If we are saved anywhere," he says, "it happens here, on this good earth, in a place."

One cannot read these sermons without being envious of the saints at First Presbyterian Church in Covington, Georgia, who heard them first. But we can be grateful that, through this book, we can all hear the gospel, spoken humbly and peacefully, but with strength and conviction, by William Wade.

Thomas G. Long

Bandy Professor Emeritus of Preaching
Candler School of Theology

Thomas G. Long is a preacher, teacher and author. He has taught at Columbia, Princeton and Erskine seminaries, and Candler School of Theology. Baylor University named him one of the top twelve most effective preachers in the English-speaking world.

Introduction

"Holiday" means "holy day", a concept that has its roots in communities where people have lived their lives according to a religious calendar. The Christian Church moves to a different rhythm than does much of society around it. That is what Advent, Christmas and Epiphany, Lent, Easter and Pentecost—all the seasons of the Church year—are about. Following the seasons of the Church year, and celebrating the high holy days, is a way we remember who we are and to whom we belong. We are reminded that this world is God's world, despite the way things often look.

Of course, Christians know that all days and seasons are holy, even those the Church calls Ordinary Time. At times through the year, the Church's high holy days converge with days that in some ways the culture around us remembers, and in some sense marks as holy. Continually, there are events in our society and the world that demand a faithful word from the pulpit. These sermons follow much of the Christian year, seeking to speak to the ways Jesus and the Scriptures challenge and guide our living of these days.

William B. Wade, Jr.

Manger Scenes

Isaiah 11:1-10; Luke 2:1-7

Christmas Eve

For some years, during the weeks leading up to Christmas, we have put this nativity set on the communion table. Most of the year it sits in a cabinet in the church parlor. A note on the shelf says it was given to the church about 1970 by Mrs. John "Becky" Buchanon. During Advent we begin bringing pieces out little by little as the Christmas story unfolds: first the angel and Mary and Joseph, then the animals and the stable, then the shepherds, and last of all, the Wise Men. Though we often get the Wise Men here for Christmas, even if the story indicates they were a little late.

I am most often the one who first takes them and arranges them on the table. I tend to spend more time than you might think setting it all up- particularly when a lot of characters begin showing up. I want to make sure it looks right. The thing is though, no matter how I leave it, I always find that someone has come along and rearranged it- at least a bit. It could be that a member of the Worship Team does it, or maybe someone else passing through the sanctuary, or maybe the custodian. Or maybe each one of those has a hand in it. It's awfully tempting.

One might do it primarily for aesthetic reasons, like arranging the flowers. What looks most attractive? Someone else might do it because it just seems reasonable: the animals should not be too close to the baby; the shepherds would surely stick together. Or, one might have a certain theological perspective: the shepherds must be closer because they are the poor; or, they all surely would stand back in awe. There are a lot of ways to look at it; there is no official diagram. But, there is a lot of power in orchestrating the nativity. One thing most everybody seems to agree upon is that the baby is center stage. All the characters look toward Jesus.

We have a number of these manger scenes at our house. Maybe you do, too. "Crèches" we tend to call them – the French word for crib. Some came to us as gifts. Others we've bought along the way. I counted three this year hanging on our Christmas tree. In the midst of Santa and reindeer and toy soldiers, we like to have them in prominent places on the tree to remind us of what's at the center of the festivities, the reason for the season, the story into which all the other stories are woven.

One of these crèches is a flat piece of wood in kind of a crescent shape. It allows the light to shine through it into the world. Another is a very crowded little stable, quaint. The third is a lean-to with just the holy family, three little round characters who remind me of the "wee people" my children used to play with and gives a whole different slant to "round yon virgin mother and child." Mary and Joseph have on red berets. I think they are French.

Behind the tree, on the window sill, sits a delicate crèche, the holy family cut out of white paper. Another is painted on wood. It's a scene from El Salvador. Mary and Joseph are Hispanic. The child reminds me of another from that place, a child some friends in our former church took into their home so he could have a heart operation. "So God imparts to human hearts the blessings of His heaven" is the prayer we sing.

In some ways, the ones I like best, are the crèches with movable pieces. One lies under our tree. It's a wooden puzzle which when lying flat, fits together inside the stable. With all the wondering and pondering the story depicts, a puzzle seems oddly appropriate. We have another scene in which the characters are made of white stone which seems to me to point not only to the life of this infant, but his sure death. Another is made of glass and sits on a little mirror in which, when you look down upon the scene, you see yourself, too. Another is a large ceramic one, sitting on the floor, because it can't sit anywhere else. The camels are almost large enough for a small child to ride, and one has tried, so one of the camels has a broken leg. Perhaps we become wise men and women mostly through our mistakes, our broken places- or at least there's the chance.

Maybe my favorite crèche though, is the one made of olive wood that I got in Bethlehem, that beautiful, wonderful, troubled little town. From time to time, the baby Jesus has gone missing, which tends to call to mind what comes only a few paragraphs later when Mary and Joseph themselves have to go looking for him.

Sometimes as I walk by one of our manger scenes, I see that the Grinch, or Frosty or Scrooge or Santa or several of them have gathered round mother and child. Sometimes I've noticed that a picture of someone in my family or of me has been sitting on the edge of that gathering. But, I don't know that that's inappropriate. Maybe it's a reminder that the story is ongoing, and we are part of it. "To you is born this day a savior," the angels say -which I take to mean us, you and me.

This night divine is not just a still scene, perfect and serene like the beautiful picture of the smiling family we send out as Christmas cards, but a cast of characters who beyond the edge of that scene, are constantly struggling with one another, with that child, and with ourselves. There are characters who are not there, someone who has died, someone who has gone away physically or emotionally. Maybe we are the ones who are not in the scene.

Or maybe, as we look upon the scene and listen to the old, old story, we can see ourselves in some way. Maybe it's in the shepherds- tough, raucous folks- hardly church people. They don't seem dressed for the occasion. They come poor, empty-handed only able to receive an inexpressible gift. It's taken a startling event to blast them out of the life they've made for themselves. Others might wonder about it- about them- but wherever they go from here, they will always be able to point back to this day, this moment. Or maybe we see ourselves as one of the shepherds who comes mostly because the others are coming- like that altar call perhaps when we were only twelve, or the confirmation class. Maybe we come only because our wife comes or our husband.

Then again, as we look, we might see ourselves in the Magi, who come not because of some sudden dramatic event-no blinding light- but rather drawn by only some distant flickering light, sometimes there, and sometimes not. Maybe we come out of intellectual curiosity more than anything else, over a long stretch of twists and turns. We hang around the edge. We enjoy the music. I remember reading of author, Walker Percy, who, in his later years, joined the confirmation class in the local church. He marched up to the front on Sunday morning- head and shoulders above the rest of the class- to finally make a profession of faith.[1]

However we have found our way to this place this day, we join a cast of unlikely characters. We come to ponder with others before us some incredible claims: that the One who lies in the manger, the One who has come into the mess and muck of our lives, is The Way and The Truth. That the One wrapped in swaddling clothes is the Resurrection and the Life; that He is the One who fills our empty places, our lonely places, our hurting places; that He is the One who forgives so much so we can forgive so little; that He is the One in whom the hopes and fears of all the years are met. You don't have

---

[1] Michael Lindvall, *Geography of God*, Geneva Press, Louisville, KY, 2001, p.7.

to understand all the doctrine; you just have to get yourself close enough to get a good look at the child.

If I Were a Wise Man: A Wise Man's Story

Psalm 72:1-10; Matthew 2:1-12

On a crisp, clear night in the desert, the stars can seem to hang so low you can almost reach out and touch them. But, part of the fascination with them is that they are always beyond us, beckoning us to a destination we can never quite reach, but to which we will forever yearn.

My ancestors studied the heavens, passing along their wisdom from generation to generation. "Magi" - magicians- we've been called. But by whatever name, what we are in our heart of hearts, are seekers. We search the deepest secrets of the universe: mathematics, physiology, philosophy, religion. We search for truth. We are interpreters of dreams, advisors to kings. It's not life so much as its meaning which directs our focus. The stars, we believe hold our destinies; they light the way to the future. The key is being able to accurately read the signs.

Oh, I've seen some amazing things in the heavens. But, one night stands out above all the rest: a star so bright all the others paled in comparison. Who could doubt it announced the coming of someone of great importance- a King of kings, a Lord of lords? It was more than curiosity that moved me, though that might well have been enough. But, it was like I had always been waiting for this. When a certain call comes in your life, you drop everything and follow, or you spend the rest of your life regretting it.

My lord gave me leave, sending others with me as an "official" delegation. We took gold, the most precious of the metals, and frankincense, the sweet perfume for priestly sacrifices, and myrrh, the bitter oil used for anointing the dead for burial- a gift for one who has power over life and death.

We packed our beasts and headed where we did not know the way. For how does one really follow a star? In the end, looking back, I tell you it was more a journey of the heart- feeling the tug, listening for guidance deep inside, which reflected the light in the sky- at least as many missteps as true ones, to be sure. But, on we went. We had never traveled so far. We feared at times that we might fall off the edge of the earth. But, some we met along the way spoke of rumors of one who was to be born and pointed us toward the capital city of the Jews. And so, we journeyed up to Jerusalem, a crossroads for traders and travelers, a battleground for many civilizations through the years, now an outpost of the Empire of Rome.

Where do you look for a king? A wise man will look in the places of power: the capitol city, the royal palace. So, we arrived at the gates and announced ourselves, and were ushered in. Wealth and position have their privileges -they garner an invitation; they allow you in behind locked gates. Evidently, we looked the part. The current monarch was one named Herod- he'd added "The Great" (I think), but it did not take long for us to realize he was not the one we sought. He ruled at the pleasure of Caesar. Herod's heavy hand had brought what passed for peace. He had built many things- marvelous buildings, mostly as monuments to himself. And though he was pleasant enough to us, he rarely looked us in the eye.

When we spoke of the star, he showed mild interest. But, when we spoke of what it might mean, he quickly called his resident theologians and instructed them to search his peoples' holy writings. They returned with bits and pieces, prophecies long since forgotten by the beautiful people of Herod's court, superstitions held only by the poor and ignorant. For who, when they have much, long for things to change? Still, after going all that way, we were prepared to follow any clues. The most promising came from an ancient prophet named Micah, who said: "But, you O Bethlehem of Ephrathah, who are little to be among the clans of Judah, from you shall come forth one who is to be ruler in Israel, whose origin is from of old, from ancient days" (5:2).

Herod was interested then. He sent us on toward Bethlehem to find any child who might fit the promise, and to send word back to him if we found the child, in order that he himself might go and pay homage. So, we set out again, though we were nearer than we had believed. The little town of Bethlehem sat only a short distance from Jerusalem, right under Herod's nose. It sits on a ridge, nestled among some hills. Its name means, "House of Bread," for all around below it are fertile fields from which the people get their bread of life. According to legend, it is the birthplace of an ancient Judean king, a shepherd boy, who fought against giants, united scattered groups of tribes into a nation and ruled the people with justice. The locals believed that one day their God would raise up another king from the same lineage, the House of David.

We sought a logical place where such a great one might be born. We asked about, but no one had heard of anything out of the ordinary; except that the village not so long before had been packed, because Caesar had ordered a census, and all the males had returned with their families to the cities of their ancestors. We had almost given up for the night when the soft cry of a young child, came to our ears. It was only a humble abode, which stood before us, a small place carved out of the limestone.

In the beginning, we never would've imagined that we would end up there. It was beyond reason. Nor would we have considered people in our position entering such a lowly place. But, in our desperation we were willing to try anything. And the tug was stronger than ever. So, we gave in to the infant's cry, and went. The entrance was so low, that we found ourselves on our knees. I tell you, it had been a long time since I'd been on my knees. But once in, I did not rise, nor did my companions.

The child lay on a straw mat like it had been taken right out of an animal trough. The two we took to be the child's parents hardly seemed surprised by our coming, as if they had already witnessed things at least as startling. And truthfully, it seemed that anyone might be welcomed there, no matter who they were or how far they had had to come. We laid before the child our extravagant gifts- which, strange to say, in that place did not seem near enough. But, I couldn't conceive of anything that would. This journey suddenly seemed more about receiving than giving. I don't know how to explain it adequately, but when I gazed upon this child, his face shown so that I believed nothing in the great darkness all around could ever overcome it. In him, it seemed that the hopes and fears of all the years were met: my hopes and fears, but the world's too.

My friends, there is no way to prove any of this to you; I can only tell you my experience. My religion has always been about how to best manage the world- or at least the part which affects me. But, maybe the truth is not about our managing the world, but our trusting in the power that does. Maybe, our destiny is not directed by the stars, but by the one who created the stars, and whose greatest power is love itself. Maybe our lives are shaped for good by how much we give ourselves to that love.

I don't know how I slipped into slumber that night, finally giving in to the strain and exhaustion of the journey, but the darkness crept back, and I shivered in my sleep. I remember the pungent smell of myrrh. Herod appeared to me, reminding me of my fears and my weakness. The faces of some I had met between Jerusalem and Bethlehem also appeared and I recalled their words uttered in low voices: "Herod is a murderous man. He murdered his wife and her mother. He murdered his three sons." It was said that it was safer to be Herod's pig than his heir. He would stand for no rivals, though Herod couldn't see that this one, I believe, could love even him.

Early in the morning, we departed, going home another way. How could we not? We set out on a different path from the one which we'd come, not knowing exactly where that would lead either, but going to tell others what we'd seen and heard.

In the days afterward, we learned of Herod's slaughter of the innocent ones. He had every male infant in Bethlehem killed- all those two years and under- just to be sure. Evil will have its day- and death, too. Hate will fight hard against love to the very end. But now, from what I've seen, I believe it will not win. Somehow, I believe, Herod did not destroy that child. Somehow, I believe, he is loose in the world.

Who's Whispering in Your Ear?
Exodus 2:1-15; Hebrews 11:23-28

I was sure somebody was going to ask me if this is going to be a Valentine message. Well, yes…kind of. The Word of God always is a message of love, even if it sometimes sounds harsh or challenging. The first Scripture this morning tells an old, familiar story, a story that is at the heart of the Hebrew Scriptures, a story told again and again by the psalmists, the prophets, the rabbis, and by parents sitting with their children and grandchildren around the table at Passover.

Listen: Exodus 2:1-15.

The second Scripture is a retelling of the story we just read, though with a little bit of a spin, or an editorial note or two that seems to happen whenever we keep passing any story from one person to another. It comes from the Letter to the Hebrews, in a section sometimes referred to as "A Great Cloud of Witnesses."

Listen: Hebrews 11:23-28.

The bookshelves in my study are cluttered with a lot of things besides books: things that were handed down to me from parents, grandparents and great-grandparents, pictures, gifts and notes from children, keepsakes from trips. They are things that remind me of many of you and others, generations of the Great Cloud of Witnesses, the Body of Christ of which we're part. These things, as you know, often give me inspiration for sermons, and encouragement in my journey of faith.

Often as I am wrestling with the sermon text, I go to reach for a commentary on my shelf to help me hear the message a little clearer, and I must push some of those items to the side to get to the book.

At one point there was a card, a card someone had written me a few years back. On the front was a copy of a famous painting, a Rembrandt; one of those where the light gently reflects off faces and hands and certain objects, making them stand out against the dark shadows of the background.

This one is the face of an old man with a long beard. One wrinkled hand clutches at his heart; the other writes in a manuscript, or at least is poised to write. His eyes stare off toward something apparently he only can see in his mind. Behind him, a young woman leans in close to his ear, her hand on his shoulder. Inside the card it reads: "Dear Billy, this is one of my favorite paintings in the current exhibit of works from The Louvre. The recorded commentary says it is a depiction of Matthew being advised by an angel as he writes his gospel. It notes that the angel is whispering in his ear, but that he cannot see her because, obviously, she is an angel. Perhaps, this will help you hear a voice when struggling with a particularly challenging sermon." I've put the card on the door of my study, if you'd like to see it.

It was Greek mythology that gave us the term, "muse," a voice whispering in the ears of writers, poets, artists and musicians. Dante, Milton, Shakespeare later spoke of muses. I imagine Rembrandt had his own muse. It's a common thought still in that regard.

But also, in a similar way, Shakespeare wrote of one behind the throne, whispering into a young king's ear from behind a curtain, giving counsel. So, we speak of somebody maybe who has the president's ear. I've watched some of those series on The Presidents on Public Television. I remember one on Harry Truman. In his memoirs, Truman wrote of the influences of his parents- some good, some bad- voices that continued to play in his head and influence the decisions he made all his life, including those as President. I hear voices too.

In this old story of Moses, passed down to us by our ancestors, we hear something of the events and the people that shaped one of the greatest leaders. Born of Hebrew slaves, by coincidence or the providence of God, depending on how you look at it, he escapes death to be raised in the household of Pharaoh himself. There he has access to learning and privilege. He is versed in the language of power, and knowledge of the system.

In the television series on The Presidents, the comment was made that great leaders often have been forged in the crucibles of difficult moments, even again and again. Moses loses everything he had in Egypt and flees to the wilderness. But it's there, it seems, he learns how to survive and thrive in sparseness, in tough conditions. He learns how to rely on ingenuity and imagination. He learns patience and trust herding sheep, things he will need for what God has in mind for him.

There is something else that intrigues me about how Moses' life was shaped. There's not a great deal said about it. In fact, you almost must read between the lines. But, I've often wondered about it. I've wondered what made Moses willing to give up all he had. What made him walk out of the palace, the good life, and risk it all? Was it just a moment of anger? What sensitized him to the situation around him, leading up to that final straw when he acted so passionately to the Egyptian beating the Hebrew?

When Pharaoh's daughter finds the baby Moses, Moses' sister, Miriam, steps out. She steps out from behind them in the safety of the bushes, risking herself, daring to ask if she can go and get a nurse from among her people to come and care for the child. And given permission, she goes and gets Moses' own mother.

What I wonder is, what was she, Moses' mother, whispering in Moses' ear as the child grew? I'm reminded of the African-American maid in the novel, *The Help*, set in the 1960's, the maid who spent more time with the white child than her mother did; who told her over and over how good and beautiful she was; and who also taught the child about the worth and beauty of others that the system around them sought to deny. She secretly told her stories and sang her songs that the child would never have heard,[2] something like those subversive songs I learned in Sunday school, like "Red and yellow, black and white, they are precious in his sight…"

I wonder about the stories Moses' mother, his nurse maid, whispered to him in the privacy of their days together, and the songs she sang to him. One of the things I carry in my head is the voice of my mother telling me, "Remember who you are. You are a child of God." When I read the psalms, or remember parts of them, I hear them in my mother's voice. I loved to hear her read. She made stories come alive. In my most uncertain times, I hear my parents saying, "Nothing can separate you from the love of God in Christ Jesus our Lord."

There are other voices in my head, of course. One is that of the mother of a friend of mine. One oppressively hot summer day when I was ten or so, she took her son and me for the afternoon. We stepped into the Miss Georgia Ice Cream Parlor in town. We'd hardly begun licking our ice cream cones when they began to melt and to run all down our faces and over our hands. I went toward the water fountain to wash off, but my friend's mother stopped me. She pointed toward a sign over the fountain that read, "Whites Only." She leaned down to me and in not so soft a voice said, "That's not right." She handed me her handkerchief and turned me around, and we stepped out the door. I've never forgotten.

---

[2] Kathryn Stockett, *The Help*, Amy Einhorn Books, Putnam Publisher, New York, 2009.

Mark Braverman is the grandson of a fifth generation Palestinian Jew. His grandfather was the direct descendant of one of the Hasidic rabbis of Europe. Many of his family have lived in the Jewish quarter of the Old City of Jerusalem. Mark often visited them there. He says that, "Sometimes -rare and precious times- you encounter someone who speaks to your heart directly…" For him, Nora Carmi was such a person. She was a Christian Palestinian who, he said, opened his eyes to the situation around him, and moved him to walk away from the life he was leading to a new one engaged in seeking justice for all God's people in the Holy Land.[3]

As we listen again to this old story of the struggle of power in Egypt, we still see it playing out on our television and computer screens and iPads, there and other places in the Middle East. I wonder who's whispering in their ears, and ours. I think of the babushkas, the old grandmothers in Russia who, when the Christian Church was suppressed by Communism, kept the faith alive by continuing to tell it to their children and grandchildren. And I take hope.

When we baptize a child, we make promises that we, parents and church members, will tell that child the good news. With all the voices that will vie for that child's attention, all that will be plugged in and streaming into his or her ears, it will take all we can do- all God can do through us. The stories of Jesus and the stories Jesus told will comfort and strengthen them for their journey. But, they will not let them or us live comfortably in the face of much the world and our society settles for. And God is relentless in trying to get our attention. Who's whispering in your ear?

When Moses had settled again, this time in Midian, where he was not so rich or powerful, but comfortable, God still did not leave him alone. God called to him one sunny day out of a bush that seemed

---

[3] Mark Braverman, *Politics of Hope.*

to burn but not burn up. And maybe, because of his mother's faithful words, he was able to recognize God's voice. And once again he followed, with the assurance that wherever he would have to go, God would always be with him.

Highs and Lows

2 Corinthians 4:3-6; Mark 9:2-9

Transfiguration Sunday

We are "stewards of mysteries," Paul says in his first letter to the Corinthians (4:1). In some ways that sounds more suited for his first century listeners than for people of the 21st century. Afterall, there is little mystery for us except what cannot yet be explained by physics or chemistry or psychiatry. Still, here we are, reading from an ancient book. We gather around a table, speaking words over 2,000 years old and professing to believe that in our communion we are raised to heaven into the very presence of Christ and surrounded on either side of us by the company of believers who've long since passed from this earth.

No wonder we've finally admitted children to the sacrament! Because, if it requires a certain abandonment of preconceptions, a certain openness to mystery, then to such as children indeed belongs the kingdom of God. It's in the receiving of the sacrament that we are offered a glimpse of the glorious power and abundant grace of the One who will sustain us in the days in-between. We are fed to sustain our journey.

Today is Transfiguration Sunday- the last Sunday before the beginning of Lent, traditionally a day for Christians to feast before we fast. It is a high before the lows. It begins on a mountain before we move into the valley. It begins with light before a time of darkness. We are told of the One in whom the glory of God shone as in no one else before or since. It's a mystery passed on to us from generations of believers before us. And if it speaks to us at all, it speaks more to our hearts than to our minds.

I suppose that every preacher, everyone who has attempted to say anything about this, has sounded a bit like Peter, babbling about something far beyond his ability to express, but feeling the need to say something anyway. If we can understand anything about this, I believe it is precisely that it has to do with "seeing" Jesus more clearly for who he is. Mark's Gospel says that what people from his hometown saw was simply Joseph the carpenter's son. They knew his people. To some folks he was a great teacher; to some he was a healer; to others he was a worker of wonders; to others still he was a blasphemer.

Mark places this event on the mountain just after Jesus has asked his disciples who people said he was. If anyone would know, certainly they would- you'd think. And they said: "Some say John the Baptist; others say Elijah; and others Jeremiah or one of the prophets" - all dead. And he asked them, "But who do you say that I am?" That's the question isn't it? Not what others say, at least not finally, but what we say- what we believe most days, what shapes the way we try to live.

Only Peter had ventured an answer to that question: "You are the Christ, the Son of the Living God," he said. The first answers, as someone has put it, were horizonal, comparisons to other people they had known or heard of, but Peter's answer is a vertical leap.[4] Jesus is not just a great human leader, another in the line of prophets, even one of them come back to life. He is the Christ, the Son of the Living God.

Then, Jesus began to talk about his suffering and death- which wasn't anything like what Peter had in mind. But, on this mountain, when Jesus was transfigured, when his appearance was dazzling, not merely that of a poor, teacher; when he held center stage between

---

[4] "God's Glory: Variations on a Theme" a sermon by Cynthia Jarvis.

Elijah and Moses, outshining them both, Peter must've felt he'd been right all along. This was a glimpse of triumph. They saw the glory of God in him. And it's Peter once again who blurts out something which might have little meaning at all, but which gives us the feeling maybe that somehow what he wanted to do was to stay in the moment: "Let us build some booths." Tents? Places of worship, to linger on that high, perhaps even to settle in on the mountain? Who knows? But, aren't we always tempted to hold on to those precious, fleeting moments of strong faith and bright hope? Times when we feel the presence of God- for truly, to most of us, they seem to be few and far between.

Maybe that wasn't such a bad thing to say. We're so used to frenetic activity. At times we need to be still and experience the presence of God. Soon enough Jesus would be taking his disciples down the mountain to a father pleading for a disturbed child and a whole crowd of hurting people, the real world. Maybe, the experience on the mountain was a sign- only a glimpse- one they often forgot it seems, but a sign nevertheless of just who it was who went before them and with them. Something to remember to hold on to or be held by- in the times of darkness and death, in the times of humiliation and hurting, so they would not lose hope.

I don't know about you, but I have times when I lose sight of that- times when grief overwhelms me, and doubt threatens me, when fear grips me. In Christ, the vertical meets the horizontal. The one who knows what it's like to be human is also the one who can help us in our weakness; the one with us and the one who also goes before us.

For the Church, this is the last Sunday before Lent- a season which begins with ashes, with a reminder of our failures, of all the ways we've messed up in life, the hopes and dreams which have been dashed. This is a time in which we're given no illusions about the pain and difficulties of life; when we're reminded of our mortality, that the days are hastening on when we will return to ashes. It's a time when what we see before us is a cross, and when we're told to bear crosses. In the Garden of Gethsemane, it will be the same three disciples Jesus takes with him to pray; Peter, James and John. But there, there will be no dazzling glory to behold, only Jesus' sweat like drops of blood before the soldiers come. There is no way around it, only through it. "Follow me," he says.

Who is this Jesus? If you're inclined to follow, or if you refuse, it is the question that really matters. Who is he? Is he only a great teacher? Just a worker of wonders? Many settle for that. Or is he the Lord of Life, the Son of the Living God? Follow me, he says. The Apostle Paul said: "We all are being changed into his likeness from one degree of glory to another" (2 Corinthians 3:18). That is, that a vision, a perception, of who Jesus is, can transfigure us- in some lesser, but important way- into something of what we are meant to be; so that we are able to experience beauty and joy and passion and love, even in the face of the darkest moments.

In a post 9/11 world, a time of terrorism, threatened by nuclear confrontation, a time of uncertainty and anxiety, we cling to a vision passed down to us by stewards of mysteries. Those who passed down to us also another vision from another hill far away: a vision of an old rugged cross where Jesus was again lifted up between two people in a place of deep darkness, but where the deep darkness could not overcome the light, and where God had the last word even about death.

No Plausible Words of Wisdom

2 Corinthians 2:1-5

Moderator's Sermon, Presbytery of Greater Atlanta

His wife gave me a lot of books and papers after he died. It was only the other day that I happened across one of his Bibles. It was filled with odds and ends, things he'd cut out or been given and had stashed away between the pages of holy scripture. There were: poems, and book marks with verses on them or made into the shape of crosses, short notes from people, funeral notices, faded newspaper articles, and old church bulletins. As I turned the pages, a wallet-sized photograph fell out - a picture of a child I recognized to be now an elder in our congregation.

"Mr. Tom," "Preacher White" some called him, served the church I currently serve. He pastored it for 22 years. He loved the people passionately, I can tell you. He was forever calling them "saints" just as the Apostle Paul called people in his churches "saints" - some whom you and I might not be so prone to see that way. This pastor was always holding up a picture of who they could be, but who also, in a deep and important sense, by the abundant grace of God, they already were. Though he did love them passionately, I can tell you also, it wasn't always easy for him. If we do it right, it can at times be a difficult thing to try to proclaim the Gospel even, and maybe especially, among people we love.

The Apostle Paul, in this part of one of his letters to the Church in Corinth, reflects on when he first came to them. Corinth was a seaport town, with a lot of action. You could find about anything you wanted to and plenty you didn't. You'd think you'd have to be a pretty slick preacher to keep their attention in Corinth, with so much else all around them promising so much. You tend to think sometimes that those early churches were made up of real saints; that they didn't have a lot of the same kind of problems our churches do today - but it isn't so. In Corinth, there was squabbling among the members. Some were even taking each other to court. There were those who were saying they were followers of Cephas, and others who said they were followers of Apollos, and others who said they were followers of Paul. Paul tried to tell them they all just belonged to Christ.

Certainly, I've been blessed to serve in the church where I am now in a small county-seat community. My family and I have been supported, encouraged, fretted over and prayed over. Members of our congregation have stood by us in sickness and sorrow and spoken words of faith when we've needed them most. I enjoy walking the streets of our community and knowing people in the stores and businesses. One of the hangouts is a local drugstore where, if you haven't gotten the day's news - I mean the real news - you can get it there.

Not too long after I moved to Covington, I was passing the drugstore, a place where locals gather for coffee and conversation, when one of the older members in our congregation, an elder, came out and greeted me. He put his arm around my shoulder and said, "Billy, I don't care what they're saying about you in there, I'll support you." I didn't quite know how I felt about that. But, over the years, I found it to be true: during difficult moments, he did support me; though at times that support came in keeping me headed in the right direction, reminding me what it means to be a preacher of the Gospel.

There's an article I have stashed away. It was printed in the *Covington News* when I first came there. It tells about my family, my former church, where I grew up, where I went to school. It all sounded harmless. It didn't say anything like: "We suspect he's going to stir some things up"; or even, "He's coming to proclaim the Gospel"; and certainly not, "He's coming to preach Christ crucified." And, I guess I was glad it didn't. It would have made me very uneasy.

When Paul came to Corinth, maybe he was remembering his time in Athens, his debates with the philosophers and scholars. But anyway, he tells the Corinthians: "When I came to you, I did not come proclaiming the mystery of God to you in lofty words or wisdom." It's a statement about content, you see, as opposed to packaging. It was not something based on his own eloquence or charm. He wasn't preaching famous words to live by or three easy steps to right belief. It wasn't even a word about how to be good or moral. He says, "I decided to know nothing among you except Christ and him crucified." That's the content.

It's not an easy word to hear. Paul has just spent a long portion of this letter talking about the foolishness of the gospel: the kind of foolishness that believes the weak will inherit the earth; that you should love your enemies and pray for your persecutors; that you should forgive the worst because you've been forgiven the worst. It's a faith based on a crucified Messiah who died precisely for those who aren't good or moral. It doesn't fit at all with the wisdom of the world. You must be changed to understand it.

We are not given a promise to make us healthy, wealthy, or even wise in the way the world is likely to understand it. Rather, it's a call to us to bear and even at times to enter difficult places with only the promise that he will never leave us; that we will be given a strength beyond our own; that we will only find our lives when we lose them. No wonder Paul says he came to Corinth with much fear and trembling with a message like that to proclaim.

I remember long ago, I was getting ready to preach one of my first sermons, and I was very nervous about it. It was my home church, my former assistant principal sat on the front row. I could remember other times I'd stood before him. A minister, who'd been preaching a while, told me it was okay to be nervous; that if you ever completely got over being nervous when you preached, you probably weren't seeing it for the holy and risky business it is. I've never forgotten that. And truthfully, I've never walked up to the pulpit when I haven't been somewhat nervous.

But often, I have to say, I'm nervous because I worry if I can keep people's attention. I worry about what people will think of me. I've worried, too, about how Jesus said, it would be better to have a millstone placed around your neck and flung into the sea than to lead someone down the wrong path. That's something to think about when you presume to speak for God. I've even worried at times that somebody might just take seriously what I have to say and then what? What if somebody believes it and takes it for the honest-to-God truth? What if somebody tells you: "because of what you said, I've decided to sell all I have and give it to the poor?" And what if they're a major contributor to the church?

I remember a man who met me at the church door after a sermon while everybody else was passing on by with pleasantries and going off to lunch. He stopped and looked me in the eyes and said: "Does this mean I need to quit my job?" He was serious. I was shocked. I didn't know what to say.

It's been said that the defining characteristic of our time is anxiety. So many people struggle with a feeling of meaninglessness. Many have found prosperity, but not peace of mind. There is a great rise in demand lately for books on spiritualism. There's a hunger which many will admit, and they're searching for something they're not finding. There's an emptiness not being filled. Paul says, "My speech and my proclamation were not with plausible words of wisdom, but with a demonstration of the Spirit and of power, so that your faith might not rest on human wisdom, but on the power of God."

There's something we're called to proclaim - to live - you and me. Not just ordained ministers. Our tradition believes Christ doesn't trust his Church just to the clergy. Every one of us is called to proclaim it; not simply because of our good training or our eloquence, nor even because of what we know, but because of whom we know; because first of all that One has touched our lives and has done for us and in us what we could not possibly have done on our own - nor even dreamed of doing. We tell it because we must, because it's a matter of life and death to us.

There is a special privilege ordained pastors still usually seem to have, a privilege given to us by a congregation, not so much because of who we are, but whom we represent; the special privilege of entering the private lives of people, and sharing some of their deepest intimacies, struggles and pains. There have been times I have not felt at all up to the task. There have been times I've gone with stammering words and faith less sure than I believed was needed. But, as the Apostle Paul asks somewhere else in his correspondence with the Corinthians: "Who is sufficient?"

Paul says, we are "commissioned by God" - something not of our own choosing, but God's - commissioned not just to preach great ideas or give clever advice, but "to preach Christ and him crucified," the greatest of paradoxes. Because if you're foolish enough to believe it, it's the sign of greatest hope, the way out of no way, the place where life has overcome the power of death. You and I are to help one another know the power of God at work within us for the sake of the world; the power to forgive, to heal, to help, to love, to be, by the grace of God, the ministers, the saints, we are called to be.

Palm Sunday Rocks

Luke 19:28-44

For many of us, Palm Sunday is one of our favorite Sundays in the Church year. We can count on a lot of energy and excitement. There will be some sort of parade- well, at least a procession. We know that the children are going to be doing their thing: waving palm branches and shouting, "Hosanna!" things we don't do a lot of in church. But, on Palm Sunday, it's just hard to put a lid on the enthusiasm. As one of the children said to me, "Mr. Billy, Palm Sunday rocks!"

By all accounts, the first Palm Sunday was a rather wild and unruly affair. It was the Festival of the Passover and Jews from all over were gathered in Jerusalem, more than at any other time of the year. The place was packed, and you know the kinds of things that happen when lots of people are crowded together.

As Jesus came riding on a donkey over Mt. Olivet in the east, like the rising of the sun, people crowded along the sides of the streets of Jerusalem. Some came out of devotion, some out of curiosity, some with high expectations, some with cherished memories, some hopeful, some apprehensive. Luke says that some of them made a path with their coats. The other gospels speak of the people carrying and spreading branches. John says they were palm branches, a traditional symbol of hospitality. Many people shouted out with loud voices. They greeted him like a king.

From the west, there was another procession that week, scholars tell us. Pontius Pilate entered Jerusalem, in all his glory, clad in armor, with horses and chariots and marching soldiers determined, by the power of Rome to make sure nothing got out of hand. The theologian, Abraham Joshua Heschel, said that religion begins in mystery, but ends in politics. [5]

Just ask Moses, sent by a voice from a burning bush to free slaves in Egypt. Just ask any of the prophets, who were always having to dodge the current administration. It didn't have to do with their private prayer life. It wasn't personal, private matters that got Jesus crucified either. He kept telling his disciples to pray alright, pray "Thy kingdom come on earth as it is in heaven." And it came in on a donkey. "Blessed is the king who comes in the name of the Lord," the people shouted. No wonder Pilate was anxious; and others too: religious leaders who'd made compromises with the government; even some disciples who were worried that all the hoopla would get the government's attention and spell trouble for Jesus and them.

"Hosanna!" they shouted, according to the gospels, which doesn't just mean, "Hooray!" It means, "Save us, now!" They were people voicing concerns not too much different from those being shouted out now in our streets: concern about government, concern about taxes, concern about jobs and wages and health care. "Jesus, save us!" they shouted.

There was a lot of misunderstanding about just what Jesus was going to do, and surely how he was going to do it. In fact, when he got near the city and saw them waving the branches, and heard them chanting, "Peace in heaven and glory in the highest," he broke down and cried, and said, "Would that even today you knew the things that make for peace."

But still, he encouraged them in their greeting. There were those around him who said, "Teacher, rebuke them. Tell them to be quiet!"

---

[5] Kristine Jane Jensen, "The Big Ditch: A Reflection on Palm Sunday", *The Presbyterian Outlook*, March 14, 2005.

But Jesus said, "Let them shout. I tell you, if these people were silent, the very stones would cry out." Isn't that a strange thing to say, the stones will cry out?

Of course, Jesus was always quoting Scripture. Maybe he was remembering how the Scripture speaks of nature itself praising God, of trees clapping their hands and mountains and hills so full of God's glory that they break forth into singing (Isaiah 55:12). "All nature sings," the old hymn goes. I remember once being in the congregation when the pastor of one of our larger churches stopped the congregation right in the middle of the processional hymn. He told us, "We're praising God. We can do better." Maybe Jesus was using an image something like, "getting blood out of a turnip" - praise out of a stone. If these people will not shout out their praises, even stones will cry out. The creation can't keep from praising God. I can say that I've listened to the babbling of brooks as the water has rolled over the rocks. There's no better praise than that. "I've cried out like Julie Andrews, "The hills are alive with the sound of music!"

I've heard other stones crying out too as I've walked through cemeteries, reading the headstones. Cemeteries are not always quiet places. If you listen, you can hear the stones. There are voices that won't stay quiet. I've stood by the remnants of the Temple Wall in Jerusalem. People go there to pray and to stuff prayers and messages among the rocks. They call the place the Wailing Wall. "The stones will cry out," he said. Maybe Jesus was thinking about something the prophet Habakkuk said when the people would not speak out against injustice. Habakkuk said, "The stone will cry out from the wall, and the beam from the woodwork respond…for the earth will be filled with the knowledge of the glory of the Lord, as the waters cover the sea."

Just off the coast of Cape Town, South Africa is Robben Island. From the 17th century until 1994 people were imprisoned there. It was a place of banishment and isolation; a place infamous for its cruelty and abuse. Political prisoners were taken there to be silenced. Its most famous inmate was Nelson Mandela, who was held there for 18 years. It's now deserted. But you can go there and walk through the halls and visit the cells. Tours are led by some former prisoners. They tell stories, but some visitors will tell you, the very stones cry out.

Maybe Jesus was thinking about what John the Baptist had told the people who came down to the Jordan River: that it wasn't their heritage or their ritual, but their heart that was important. "I tell you," he said, God is able from these stones to raise up children of Abraham" (Matthew 3:9).

"Tell these people to be quiet," some of the religious leaders told Jesus. There are always those who have a stake in the status quo, people trying to cement their own place of status, or privilege, or power. Not long before this, Jesus encountered a blind man named Bartimaeus, who was begging on the street. Crowds were gathered in Jericho to greet Jesus as he entered the city. When Bartimaeus called out to Jesus for help, people in the crowd told Bartimaeus to be quiet. But he would not be silent and cried out louder. And Jesus encouraged him.

When Martin Luther King, Jr. was jailed in Birmingham, in his now famous letter, he confronted his colleagues, white and black, for staying silent and saying it was not the time for speaking out and challenging the system. Jesus said the very stones would cry out.

The Kingdom is coming. It's not what a lot of people think. It will turn some things upside down: the last will be first, the first last; swords will be beaten into plowshares; there will be peace beyond our understanding. If we look, we will see glimpses; if we listen we might hear voices. There are those, I tell you, who have so experienced the love of God in their lives, who have so experienced the forgiveness God offers and the hope God holds out, that they simply won't be quiet. If you give them half a chance, they'll tell you their story. If you can see at all, they'll show you their lives. There are plenty around here, in this crowd.

On that first Palm Sunday, Simon Peter was in the crowd. A little earlier, when Jesus had asked his disciples who they said he was, Peter blurted out, "You are the Christ!" Simon was often speaking out loudly, sometimes before he thought things through very well. But, Jesus called him, The Rock, "Petra," and said that on him would he build his Church.

Not long after this parade in Jerusalem, there were few voices crying out to Jesus or even admitting they knew him. Even Peter was silent. But, only a few days later, from the silence of a tomb, some rocks began to shake and roll and clatter, to cry out loud enough to wake the dead.

Maundy Thursday

John 13:1-17, 34-35

Community Holy Week Services

"A new commandment I give you," Jesus said. That's where this day, "Maundy Thursday" gets its name, from the Latin word "mandate," which means "commandment." The context of it is The Last Supper, which is a little different in John's gospel than in the others. The others all have the disciples sitting around the table with Jesus. But only John has this stuff about Jesus washing the feet of the disciples.

Maybe one of you other preachers should have preached on this text today. I mean, it's a strange text for Presbyterians, and we tend to avoid it if we can. Most of us would rather do about anything than engage in foot washing, particularly in church. Oh, we will spend hours baking pies for fellowship suppers, or building houses for people who can't afford them, or taking people to the doctor when they can't get themselves there, or teaching people to read. We'll even try to sing a few new hymns- once in a while- and endure a few vocal "amens" on occasion, but please, please don't ask us to take off our shoes in church.

I asked our folks once to consider it. You would've thought I'd asked them to be immersed or something. I think that's kind of the idea Peter had when, sounding like a Baptist, he said finally to Jesus, "Then wash me from head to toe." But Jesus said, "No, just your feet will do." So, I think we Presbyterians have got something right. We're just working at the wrong end is all.

I think the problem for us is, we just don't like to be that familiar with each other. We don't want to be that exposed. There are some things people don't need to know about us. We'd rather other folks see just our more beautiful places. You know that part of Isaiah, where the prophet says, "Beautiful upon the mountains are the feet of those who bring good news?" He obviously was speaking symbolically. Even our most fundamentalist members know you can't take everything in the Bible literally. Who takes Jesus' words about money literally? Same thing about feet.

When Paul was talking to the Corinthians about treating our unpresentable parts with greater modesty, he was talking about feet- at least old feet. You see, it's not that I haven't ever participated in a foot-washing. I've experienced a few, mainly at youth conferences. Young people don't usually have the crooked toes and bunions and toenail disease we tend to get as we get older, and young people do not tend to mind touching each other a little more.

I especially remember a time when I was in South Africa. I was about thirty years old, so it was a while ago. South Africa was still living under the apartheid system. The small white minority ruled the government and controlled the businesses. People of color had to live out from town in poor settlements called townships, which wasn't all that different from neighborhoods where I grew up. Anyway, some things at that time were just beginning to crack, a little bit. There were hints of change, though hardly anybody could see it happening without a great deal of violence.

One of those glimpses of change came in a church conference- a youth conference. A small group of us from our Presbyterian denomination here had been invited by Presbyterians there. There were black and white young people in our group and in the South African group attending the conference, which was very unusual. Doesn't it seem that often young people are the ones most open to the new directions of the Holy Spirit? We'd been together a couple of weeks when one of the leaders of the conference set up a foot-washing as part of our evening worship service. We were instructed to wash the feet of whoever happened to be seated next to us. Here were people who rarely were together at all- mostly as boss and hired help- washing each other's feet. Some were literally in tears, these folks who were so separated legally, socially, economically, realizing for the first time really, that they were sisters and brothers in Christ.

"He laid his garments aside and girded himself with a towel and began to wash their feet," and he said, "A new commandment I give you, that you love one another, even as I have loved you." Truthfully, I have wished oftentimes that there was another way, rather than the way of serving. I don't know about you, but I tend to prefer upward mobility. Most often I come to church to get my needs met, to find ways for self-improvement. I like sitting at the head table. I like being first in line, or at least close to it. I enjoy having access to people in the right places. I enjoy being able to pick up the check. I like feeling important.

I wish there were another way, because I'm often in hot pursuit of happiness, and I don't want to suffer. I want to avoid pain. I want an easier life. I wish there were another way than having to love the unlovable and the unloving. Sometimes I really want revenge- not necessarily violently, but at least cleverly. I have a hard time understanding power in weakness, gaining our lives in losing them. Do you? I often wish there were another way. But this week, when we hear Jesus say, "Follow me," there's no denying where we are headed. It's toward a cross. The issue is not one of self-improvement, but salvation, new life altogether.

In the new fellowship to which he calls us, it doesn't matter what we do for a living, or how much money we make, or how sophisticated we are. It doesn't matter what position we hold, or where we went to school, or what grades we've gotten, or what degrees we have. It doesn't matter what mistakes we've made, or what sins we've committed. The only thing that matters is if we believe him when he says, "A new commandment I give you, that you love one another as I have loved you." It only matters if we really understand that he loves us as he loved those first disciples whom he bent down to serve- even Judas- washing their dirty feet, cleaning their ugly places. It only matters if we "get it," in here, in our hearts, that he loves all of us, that he will stoop to the lowest places, go to the greatest depths for us.

Once, not long ago, I was struggling to make sense of some things in my life, feeling very low. A friend came to the door of my study, a pastor from another congregation, a congregation a lot different from my own. We sat and talked a while. Mainly, he listened, offering no advice for how to improve my life, but sharing some difficult places in his own life. Then he said, "We have a tradition in our church. If you don't mind, I'd like to offer it to you." He got down on his knees in front of me and took a handkerchief, and as my tears fell on my feet, he began to wipe them with the handkerchief as he prayed for God to wipe the dirt from my life, and to bathe me in Christ's redemption and love.

"Do you know what I have done to you?" Jesus asked. "If I, your Lord and teacher, have washed your feet, you also ought to wash one another's feet... If *you* know these things, blessed are you if you *do* them."

Good Friday
John 18:28-40

Community Holy Week Services

I am grateful to First Methodist Church for hosting us this year. We have a long tradition in this community of gathering together for Holy Week and Thanksgiving. I know it's not easy for some of you to come out in the middle of the day for this, to get away from work and other things in your busy schedules. Doing so says something about how important you think this week is for you, and maybe for the world.

What I've said over and over to our people through the years is that we seek to move to a different rhythm than does much of society around us. That's what Holy Week and Lent and Advent and Epiphany and Pentecost -all the seasons of the church year- are about. They remind us that there is more going on than what we often tend to think about in all our busyness and striving, in the things in which we often invest our time and energy and attention. We are reminded that we are God's people and that this world is God's, despite the way things often look.

Today, of course, is called "Good Friday," though a lot of folks have trouble understanding why it could be called "good." You don't get the crowds on Friday you tend to get on Sunday. Which really reflects what happened on the first Good Friday, when so many of those who gathered along the road just a few days before shouting "Hosanna!" by Friday had gone their way.

I remember years ago, when I was first starting out in ministry. I was a campus minister at Auburn. I decided we needed a Good Friday service among the Presbyterian students and friends at the center there. It was just a little group that gathered out in the yard around a bare rugged cross. We'd hardly started when there was a clap of thunder and it began to pour rain. Some ran immediately for shelter. Several of us stood there not knowing what to do. But finally, all of us left. I looked back at the cross standing by itself in the rain.

Unlike some of the other days of Holy Week, it's not hard to figure what Jesus is doing on Friday. The hard part about preaching on Friday is trying to decide just where to focus. The cross, of course, but it's a long story getting there. The cross makes a lot of folks uncomfortable. Some churches, you'll notice, don't display them very evidently, for that reason. But, without the cross, there is no Gospel. Without the cross, there is no Easter.

On Good Friday, some preachers just read the whole story from Matthew, Mark, Luke or John, and let it go at that. And, maybe that is the best thing to do, because that's often the only time some of us are going to hear it. But, I've been asked to preach, so I'm going to take just a portion of John's gospel as the text.

This comes after Jesus has been arrested in the garden, where Peter had drawn his sword and cut off the ear of the servant of the high priest- for which, Peter was not arrested. It's after Jesus is taken to the high priest, while Peter stands outside and denies he's a disciple of Jesus, which is obviously the truth at that point. It's after they then led Jesus to the praetorium, to Pilate, to crucify Jesus, while they stood outside so they would not defile themselves.

Listen: John 18:28-40.

It all seems a little much, don't you think, putting him to death? What in the world could possibly be the reason for that? Why not just ignore him? I really haven't experienced a great deal of threat in my life for claiming to follow Jesus. Mostly people in our society just don't seem to see Christianity as relevant. So, I keep wondering what stirred up these people. How did they see Jesus as a threat? Surely, they recognized Jesus' kingdom didn't have anything to do with this world. It had nothing to do with politics. It was just about what happens in the hearts of individuals. It was just about our own personal relationship with Jesus, just Jesus and me. What's the threat?

Yet he is crucified on a Roman cross, a punishment reserved for political criminals. Pilate kept telling them to just let it go. Jesus says, "My kingdom is not of this world. If my kingship were of this world, my servants would fight [for me]." Odd, considering how often wars have been fought, violence committed in Jesus' name.

"So, you are a King," Pilate says. Jesus says, "You said it…I came into the world to bear witness to the truth. Everyone who is of the truth hears my voice." And Pilate says, "What is truth?" Sound familiar? What's so threatening about the truth? We all have our truth. We listen to the voices we want to hear. What is truth? Pilate couldn't see it even as it stood right in front of him. He wasn't alone in that. The truth is in Jesus' life and death, and what God does with that, in that.

The government officials, of course, just wanted to keep the peace. That's nothing to make light of; it's what we often settle for. It has little to do with real justice. It's a matter of who has the power. Jesus kept drawing crowds, and some people were calling him a king; and Pilate wanted to keep a lid on things. Pilate says to Jesus, "Don't you know I have the power to release you or to crucify you?" Pilate thought he had the power. But that isn't the truth.

John's gospel doesn't tell us this, but the other gospels say that when Jesus was tempted by Satan in the wilderness, Satan offered him the whole world if Jesus would just bow down and serve him. What he was offering, in effect, was the same old, same old, the usual ways of operating in the world, the same old ideas of what makes for might and power and peace. But Jesus refused to be that kind of Messiah. What Jesus was bringing was a different kind of peace, beyond our understanding. It's the truth which Jesus shows us in himself, reconciling us to God and to one another.

There were the religious leaders, the ones with all the degrees and credentials, suspicious of an itinerant preacher who kept coloring outside the lines. What seminary did you attend? Who authorized you, Jesus? He healed people on the Sabbath. He contradicted Moses: "An eye for an eye…But I say, 'Love your enemies, pray for your persecutors'." He hung around the wrong people, and confused their notion of who is good: A Samaritan you say, an example to us? Jesus said the greatest of all is the servant of all. The world sees all this as nonsense, and plenty of us who claim to follow Jesus really think he must be a bit naïve. I mean, how far can you really take this stuff, right?

Obviously, Jesus took it to the cross. You must lose your life to gain it, he said. You must die to some things to awake to the new life, the abundant life he offers. His weapon of choice was the cross, and he told all who would follow him to pick up our own crosses.

On Sunday he came humble, riding on a donkey. Those who hoped for a king went to greet him. Some had heard he'd raised the dead, but you know how some people will believe anything. On this Good Friday, I believe, the question for us is whether we will trust the One who promises to overcome evil with good; who proclaims a God who brings good out of the worst. The question for us is whether that is the truth, if the life he lived is the Truth.

He doesn't avoid evil or death, nor does he promise that to those who would follow him. He forges into the lonely depths of hell itself for those who've left him, betrayed him, nailed him to a cross. "While we were yet sinners, Christ died for us" (Romans 5:8). He goes to a cross not because a cross is what God demanded. It's not God's plan. God's plan is the way Christ takes it on, for sinners, for us. Violence is our own doing. It's the price God pays for loving us, for God so loved the world.

Like the little service drowned out by the rain, this whole story looks like it has a sad, pathetic ending. It's what happens to the least, the powerless. What in the world would you expect? Unless…unless what Jesus proclaimed is the Truth. Unless the world can't really stamp him out. Unless there will be other little truths spreading around too.

If we believe what Jesus says, God is defined in him. God works this way in the world and calls us to live this way. It will challenge the powers in this world. It will threaten the foundations of the society we have built. It will call us into a new community. It is this God whom we're called to trust here and now and beyond what we yet can see.

The Last Laugh

John 20:1-18

Today is April first. I suspect that a lot of preachers are taking note of that today. The last time Easter fell on April first was 1956. Despite what some of you might think, I was too young to preach in 1956. The next time Easter falls on April first will be over a decade from now and I might be too old to preach. So, it's just too much to resist saying something today about Easter being on April Fool's Day.

After all, the Apostle Paul said we are "fools for Christ" (1 Corinthians 4:10). What we proclaim as Gospel is heard by many as nonsense. It's often hard to swallow even for those of us who call ourselves followers of Christ. It can seem a foolish way to live if we take Jesus seriously. Jesus talked about the kingdom of God. He told stories that ended with a twist: the first were last, the last first; insiders were outsiders, outsiders were insiders; good people were bad, bad people good. If you didn't laugh, you'd cry. When Jesus went to the cross, Pilate had written over Jesus' head: "The King of the Jews." It was meant to be a joke.

It was still dark when Mary Magdalene came to the tomb, John says; and we can't help but remember the opening of John's gospel, about the light that the darkness has not overcome. But she had been there-on "Good" Friday. She was one of the only ones there, as he died, bleeding on the cross. She'd watched them raise the sponge to his lips, heard that last horrid gasp of breath and his final cry: "It is finished." The light went out. "There's nothing surer than death and taxes," they say. At our best, we just learn to cope. How many of us have made trips back to the cemetery as part of our saying goodbye? Maybe we've stood there pouring out our hearts in sorrow or maybe anger, talking to one who could no longer talk back. A counselor will tell us it's part of the grieving process. Get it out and be done with it. You must learn to let go- let go and move on. She would never forget him, could never forget him. At least, no one can take your memories.

But, they can disturb your memories, desecrate your hallowed ground. I remember visiting an old family cemetery and was shocked to see the damage vandals had done, writing graffiti and knocking over stones. No respect for the dead or the grieving. Mary Magdalene saw the stone out of place, rolled away from the tomb, and went immediately to tell the others the only thing she could imagine had happened: "They've taken the Lord out of the tomb, and we don't know where they've laid him." A cruel prank?

Then Peter and another disciple, "the one Jesus loved," we're told - whom we suppose was John, the author, since he calls him Jesus' favorite- Peter and the "beloved one" come running like children in a foot race. John is leading but he stops and investigates the tomb, seeing the clothing lying there, but no body. Peter, always full speed ahead, rushes into the tomb. Then the other disciple goes in after him. The other disciple "sees" and "believes," though we don't know quite what he believes since we're told they didn't yet know the scriptures. They didn't know that he "must rise from the dead." Then, they just go home. What else could they do? Where else was there to go?

But Mary stays. Nadia Bolz-Weber, a stand- up comic before God called her to preach, (speaking of jokes), is the pastor of House for All Sinners and Saints, a church full of outcasts and recovering addicts. She says she has a tattoo of Mary Magdalene covering half of one arm. She says Mary Magdalene is the "patron saint of just showing up." [6] John's gospel states that Mary Magdalene was at the foot of the cross when Jesus died and the first one to the tomb on the third day. When Peter and the other disciple leave, Mary stays, crying outside the tomb.

Then she stoops to look in. She sees two angels inside, who must have been taking a break when Peter and the other disciple went inside the tomb. But they're back. They don't say what we're used to hearing: "He is not here. He is risen!" No, they simply ask why she is crying- like that would be an odd thing as this point. Now, I don't know how dark it still is by this time, but it has not yet dawned on Mary Magdalene what has happened. There is still no body there and no evident explanation for his being gone. It makes no sense to her.

Then, she turns around and sees someone standing there who also asks her why she's crying and whom she seeks. She supposes he can help her find Jesus, not knowing Jesus has found her. She takes him for the gardener, the caretaker, his regular Jesus clothes being back in the tomb. He's found new clothes. And in a sense, he is the gardener; he is the caretaker. For, his garden is the kingdom of God, the seeds of which have been planted in our midst, being scattered across the world to blossom in abundance. He is the caretaker, the one who serves and can be found taking care of the neediest. "When did we see you?" they asked the judge in Jesus' story. You remember. The judge said, "I was among the least." Neither those who responded nor those who didn't had recognized him.

John doesn't say what had first drawn Mary Magdalene to Jesus, but when he calls her by name, she knows who it is. John says the shepherd knows his sheep by name; when he calls them, they recognize his voice. In baptism, our names are called, and we are

---

[6] Nadia Bolz-Weber, *Pastrix: The Cranky, Beautiful Faith of Sinners and Saints.* Jericho Books, Nashville, 2013, p. 198.

reminded that we are all children of God. We are, each of us, his beloved ones.

When all she could see was death, the Resurrection and the Life called her by name: "Mary." Why Mary? Why not someone of more importance? Well, he was always coming to those little known or remembered: poor beggars, prostitutes, tax collectors. What he has spoken has always been a surprise, a twist, poking fun at what we usually expect to see or hear. His parables are really jokes he hopes we'll get- but we're a tough audience.

"Teacher," she says to him. Then, she must have reached out to hold him. She has him back, not wanting to let loose. It's what all of us want when we have loved someone and lost that person. He is the same, but different. He is not just a memory, but a real presence. There is no body left in the tomb. The gospels have gone to great lengths to speak of his walking, eating, touching. A memory would not have changed Mary or the disciples into those willing to pick up their own crosses and follow. "Don't hold on to me, Mary," he says, for he is moving on, loose in the world.

Mary Magdalene is no one, except one he loves. The risen Christ comes to her in her grief and helplessness and calls her by name, and Mary Magdalene, this lowly woman, becomes the first witness to the Resurrection, the first preacher of the Gospel.

Somewhere I remember seeing a painting of Jesus coming out of the tomb- if not laughing, at least with a broad grin on his face. Christian theologian Jurgen Moltmann said, "With Easter the laughter of the redeemed…. begins." [7] It is the greatest twist, the biggest surprise, the last laugh- appropriate on April Fool's Day. It is central to the Gospel. Without the resurrection, there is no Gospel to preach. Paul

---

[7] Jurgen Moltmann, *The Passion for Life: A Messianic Lifestyle.*

said: "If Christ has not been raised, we are of all people most to be pitied" (1 Corinthians 15:19). But rejoice! Dance! Laugh! It's not those who seem to run the world who really run it. It is the one who was crucified, dead and buried, and whom God raised; and who calls us, a bunch of seemingly nobodies, to be his body in the world, doing what seems naive and impractical, what seems foolish in the world, but is the power of God.

"Don't hold on to me," he says; as he heads out before us. But in his everlasting love he promises to hold on to us, so that nothing can separate us from him. Out in the garden, the garden here at the church where some of our loved ones are buried, it is written in stone: "I will come and take you to myself, that where I am, you may be also" (John 14:3). The Resurrection begins here as we learn to live as Easter people in the world God so loves, until Jesus takes us to be with him and leads us to the day when God will transform all creation and there will be a new heaven and a new earth. No fooling.

Gone Fishing
John 21:1-19

Last Sunday was "Low Sunday," as Larry and Patrick told us. Not the official name given by the Church, but usually noted nonetheless. We really didn't have to be told, we could just look around us. It's called Low Sunday because it often stands in stark contrast to the high of Easter, not only the music and song and pageantry, but its high hopes and full pews. "He is risen!" the crowd roars on Easter Sunday. On the Sunday after, we must shout to get one another's attention to pass the attendance register.

A friend sent me a picture of a church sign out in front of its building last week. The sign said: "Pretend it's Easter and come back this Sunday. After all, He's still alive." It reminds me of the little boy who was asked by his aunt how church was that first Sunday after Easter. He said: "The preacher told us, 'Jesus is not here, he's gone before us.'" After Easter, those first disciples were gone, too. On the third Sunday of Easter, the Church offers up this story, a story of a Jesus who goes to find them.

Listen: John 21: 1-19.

You've seen the bumper sticker on the back of the pick-up truck or hanging in the store window: "Gone Fishing." This week it could be the message on the church sign. It was Peter who said it. He never seemed to be easy just sitting still- not much of a contemplative. He had to work things out- literally. As usual, the others followed him, or at least as many of them as still seemed to be together and knew how to fish: Thomas, Nathaniel, James and John, and two others John doesn't seem to quite remember. They'd gone to do some thinking – or not do some thinking; gone maybe for a little emotional space. Or maybe they were going back to where it all began; going back to where they'd first met Jesus, who'd called to them from the shore when they'd been working on their boats, and their lives had suddenly taken a new direction. It hadn't turned out as they'd thought and what was now before them, they couldn't imagine. What next? All they knew was what they'd always done, so they go back to it. But it could never be the same again.

In fact, they fish all night and catch nothing, zilch, nada. Then, just as a new day is breaking, they hear a voice calling from the shore: "Cast your net on the right." There's something awfully familiar about this. Luke tells us a very similar story back before Jesus' crucifixion. Maybe it's the same story; maybe it's the same thing, but different, in the light of the resurrection. They cast their nets again, this time on the right side. And it fills so full of fish the disciples can't haul them all into the boat. The disciple whom Jesus loved, John, (at least according to- John), the one whom Peter had raced to the empty tomb, cries out: "It is the Lord!" He has come to find them. In the story in Luke, Peter had backed away from Jesus, telling Jesus to get away from him because he was a sinful man. But this time, Peter springs into the water and heads toward the one on the shore.

There is a charcoal fire and Jesus is cooking breakfast. He tells them to bring more fish. Simon Peter wades back into the water where the others have brought the boat, and hauls in the full net by himself. Then Jesus gives them bread and fish, and they all know it's the Lord. John's gospel says this is the third time Jesus was revealed to the disciples after he was raised.

It seems Jesus might appear anywhere, during Monday work while we're counting our profits, when we're on the beach with friends, while we're at the breakfast table. Maybe not quite like he appeared to those first disciples, but with us nonetheless. The stories of Jesus' appearance are an assurance of Christ in the world and with us. That he appeared three times to his closest disciples and each time they had a hard time recognizing him might be comforting to us in our own difficulty recognizing his presence with us in our lives. Maybe, like the dawning of the light, it dawns on us gradually – not all at once, but through glimpses here and there, just when we start to forget; when the darkness begins to creep back in on us, or to flood over us; when our nets are empty, and we have no idea where to cast them. Christ with us, feeding us, nourishing us, sustaining us in our weakness and strengthening us for his work in the world.

When they'd finished breakfast, Jesus said to Peter: "Do you love me more than these?" "These" what? These other disciples? Maybe he says it to Peter because Peter has always kept trying to outrun and outswim the others, to be first to Jesus. But, in this curious story, maybe he means, do you love me more than these fish? That is, more than this life of fishing, even the kind of fishing which could yield a catch like this one. Peter, can you give up this old life for a new one? It will be risky. Love offers no security. But it is more abundant for those who can see. Peter, do you love me? he asks. Three times Jesus asks him, which echoes the three times Peter denied him- not to underscore Peter's weakness, his faithlessness, but to offer him absolution, forgiveness and empowerment. "Hear this Peter. Hear this Peter. Hear this Peter." Let it sink in.

When Peter says, "Yes Lord, you know I love you," Jesus says, "Feed my sheep." Care for my people. He doesn't give up on Peter, as he doesn't give up on any of us. Jesus entrusts his ministry to this one who'd betrayed him- whom he'd at one time called, Satan. The Church is full of people like him, but we are by God's grace, Christ's body in the world.

It's not so much a matter of professing something with our lips, as living a life, the life he lives. Often we confess our faith with some theology or doctrine we have yet to get just right- getting all our "i's" dotted and our "t's" crossed; trying to make sure we're good enough to get into heaven. We spend so much time and energy defining our boundaries – who's in and who's out- and determining who's worth our effort and our love. When did we see you Lord? When you did it to the least, he says- at the last judgement (Mt.25). "Feed my sheep," Jesus says, to Peter. That's the heart of it. Feed my sheep with the same power you're given to catch an unbelievable amount of fish.

Jesus comes to find us, to send us out into the world in his name. It's been suggested that 153 fish symbolize the number of kinds of fish they believed there were in the world, and thus the net symbolizes one which catches all varieties for the fisher of human beings- all varieties of peoples, all nations, caught and held by the grace of God. "Feed my sheep" –as I have fed you. After breakfast on the beach, he says: "Do this and remember." And whenever you do it, I will be there. Open your eyes and see.

A New Community
Acts 2

Pentecost marks the coming of the one John the Baptizer said would baptize us with the Spirit and with fire. While the season of Lent begins with ashes, the season of Pentecost begins with a blazing fire. Timid disciples become bold apostles. The Spirit breathes life into a newborn Church.

There's a lot of noise at Pentecost. Most of us are more familiar, and likely more comfortable, with a God who comes not in the earthquake, or the wind, or the fire, but in the still small voice, preferably inside us. We are used to praying for the One who will calm our storms, not the One who will stir things up and rock our boat. We desire the One who soothes, not the One who unsettles. We seek the One who builds up and brings together, not the One who tears down and scatters. So, Pentecost does not come easy for God's frozen chosen.

It's no wonder it is Luke who tells this story. Luke passes along Jesus' stories that turn things upside down, that shatter all our preconceived notions of first and last, greatest and least; of those who are " in" and those who are " out," those who are sick and those who think they are well, those who are blind and those who really see, those who are deaf and those who hear, those who are prodigals and those who believe they are righteous, those who are enemies and those who are truly neighbors. In Luke's gospel, God is continually doing a new thing.

This is not the only Pentecost story in the Bible. John also has one, where the Risen Jesus comes to the disciples who are shut up together in a house, hiding in fear of what might happen to them. Jesus comes to them and says, "Peace be with you" (the original

Passing of the Peace). He says, "As the Father has sent me, I send you." The "disciples" become "apostles"; those who have been learning and practicing are now those who are sent in Jesus' name.

When Jesus said this, he breathed on them and said to them, "Receive the Holy Spirit." It's a quieter, calmer kind of Pentecost, but one thing is the same: the breath of God that was breathed into the first humans to give life, is breathed again into the disciples to make a new creation. They, in turn, are to breathe that new life into others throughout the world.

You see, wind and breath and spirit are the same words in the biblical languages. I like the Hebrew, "ruach." It's God's breath, the breath of the Risen Christ, that blows through those at the Festival of Pentecost, as Luke tells it, warming up those frozen, lifeless disciples, and moving them to take the Good News to all the world.

It's not that we ever have the Spirit, but that the Spirit has us. The Spirit blows where it wills, we're told. You can as easily grasp the wind. The Spirit at Pentecost gives voice to women and servants, to all kinds of people to whom nobody much listened. The Holy Spirit took some unremarkable people and turned them into eloquent and bold witnesses, the least becoming some of the greatest.

I remember sometime back, when our community was talking some about what to do for people who are homeless among us. Nobody really was doing much of anything rather than passing them on to be someone else's problem. Except Clara Lett and her little church, who kept running into one obstacle after another while trying to follow the One who continues to make a way out of no way. A group of folks gathered at the library, speaking in quiet voices.

The powers that be said it would be nice for somebody to do something, and no doubt helpful for the city and the county in some ways, but there were all kinds of restrictions and regulations and really no money to use. During all this, there were some people who began to speak. It was a while before I realized, that those speaking so passionately and poignantly, were people who had lived at the small shelter in Porterdale, and some who had gone through rehab programs, and had been given new life, and who thanked God for it. Some others of us then began to hear and understand for the first time. It seemed to me I could feel the slight stirring of a breeze.

It is the Spirit that stirs us, so that we, too, cannot just sit behind our doors, tending to our own business, waiting for someone else to do something. It's the Spirit who moves us out of our comfort zones to places we often would rather not go, to provide for God's children who need a place to sleep, and food to eat, and someone to tell them they are loved, that they matter, really matter, to God and also to those of us who bear Christ's name.

The Holy Spirit is what makes us the Church. There was no Church before Pentecost. It is the Holy Spirit who gives strength to walk and not faint; who gives us faith to tread where we can't see the way; who gives us the words when we don't know what to say; who interprets the groans of the world and our sighs too deep for words. It's the Holy Spirit who enables us to dream dreams and see visions of the amazing things God is doing in the world and calls us to help in that work.

Frank Schaeffer, son of world-known evangelical leader, Francis Schaeffer, tells about making a film in South Africa in the late `80s, when the people still lived under apartheid. It was, he admits, a third-rate film. He was broke and struggling to find his way, to find who he was. The movie was supposed to be set in Miami, but they filmed it in South Africa to save money. They were shooting in an abandoned railroad yard in Pretoria. It was a cold, winter day and the hundred or so black African extras were gathered around a fire to stay warm between takes. They had been hired for a few rand and a hot meal.

Schaeffer says he told them to start marching around the fire and singing, singing anything as long as their lips were moving. Later they would dub in something to make it sound like a demonic ritual. They got up and began to sing, "Shosho Loza," a hymn that was once sung by the black gold miners who were missing their homes and families. It had more recently been adopted by the African National Congress as a kind of unofficial hymn of resistance. It was considered subversive.

If you have ever heard it, you know it is a hauntingly beautiful song. The many extras, from various places and tribes in South Africa, none of whom knew each other before they were hired for the film, and who spoke various dialects, sang as if they had rehearsed for weeks. They sang in harmony echoing around the railyard, with the flames from the fire dancing on the heads of their shadows. Some of the white crew members got nervous and said they better get them to stop. But, a few of the crew joined in. Schaeffer says it was the most beautiful thing about that pitiful movie, and they were going to cut it out. Those people sang like angels, the bass voices sounding as sweet as French horns, the women's voices harmonizing in tones to break your heart- and maybe then, to begin to heal it.[8]

Pentecost, thank God, is at least an annual thing for the Church. Most of it for us is scripted, but sometimes the Spirit breaks in among us. The Holy Spirit keeps coming to shake us up, to awaken dead lives; to fan once again the flames in churches where the

---

[8] Frank Schaeffer, *Crazy for God*, Carroll and Graf Publishers, New York, 2007, pp. 370-371.

passion has been expiring; to stir us from our lethargy and move us toward surprising new venues of ministry.

The chatter of voices so common to our gathering for worship each Sunday seems particularly appropriate for Pentecost. Pentecost has been called "a miracle of communication." [9] What a blessing for times like these. The Spirit comes, reminding us that the Church belongs to God, and that it's the Christ of Christianity who is the Lord and Savior of all. We are reminded that the Almighty God speaks in many languages. Those who gathered on the first Pentecost, who came to the ancient festival from places where they had been scattered, had the Gospel spoken in their own language, for the language of God is the language of love.

In this congregation we've had a number of people who've come to us from other places around the world. The Holy Spirit calls us into a new community where there is no longer just "us and them"; where we hear new voices and learn new things God speaks through others who also are a part of the Body of Christ in their own unique ways. The Spirit calls into a community where together we become more the Church God desires us to be, for the world God so loves.

---

[9] Jason Byassee, "The Holy Spirit's New World Order, *Journal for Preachers*, Pentecost 2018, p. 15.

All Dogs Go to Heaven?
Genesis 7:1-5; 9:8-13; Romans 8:18-24

I lay in the grass in the sunshine of a warm midwinter day. There wasn't a cloud in the sky. Beside me—a good arm's distance away – I watched a colony of ants. Known for their industriousness and cooperation, they are studied in computer science and robotics for their problem- solving ability. In certain parts of Africa, ants have been considered messengers of the gods.

I shielded my eyes from the bright light and looked down the hill toward the lake. There were a couple of small boats. Ducks and geese swam in the water. A hawk screeched, and seagulls circled in the sky. Cows grazed on the opposite bank. At the bottom of the hill silhouetted against the shimmering water, was my wife of 34 years, my grandson of 7 years, my dog of almost 17 years.

She still runs to meet me when I pull into the driveway—the dog, I'm talking about—and greets me with a weak, hoarse bark that's known better days. She nuzzles her head against my leg, and I lean down to hug her. We've had to start putting her inside on cold days lately and feeding her special food. She trips now sometimes going up and down stairs. Her eyesight's not very good and she can't hear a lick. She sleeps so soundly sometimes I wonder if she's alive. I come right up on her and touch her. She startles and struggles to her feet to show me she's still on duty.

There are currently twice as many pets in American households as children under 18. Certain animals become much like part of our family. Often, we go to great lengths and spend a lot of money caring for them. And when they die, we grieve. A friend of mine laments that in seminary we were given no training in providing pastoral care for people in relation to their pets.[10] But maybe we should have. Animals can find a pretty important place in our lives. It's not unusual for people and their pets to begin to look alike—even to act something alike, which sometimes is better for the person than the pet.

People do all kinds of things with and for their pets. Some offices have "Bring Your Pet to Work Day." You can take your dog to a Braves Game on "Bark in the Park Day." There's a doggie U-tube site and now "Tweets for Dogs." Of course, there are pet shows where we can show them off. In the paper the other day, I saw a picture of Larry Kennon. The caption read, "Most Handsome Male." But it applied to his dog, Barnabas, apparently; named of course for the Apostle Paul's beloved companion on the Gospel trail.

Now, some people, I believe, take it way too far: putting their pets in their wills and taking out large insurance policies on them, pampering and spoiling them. Some pets live far more comfortable lives than many people throughout the world. But, still, there can be something very special about our bond with an animal.

Maybe that's always been so. But, many of us have grown up with stories of Timmy and Lassie, Roy Rogers and Trigger, Flipper and .... whoever the kid was. Disney has flooded our hearts with *The Incredible Journey* and *Old Yeller*, and animated characters like Mickey Mouse, Donald Duck, The Lion King and Jiminy Cricket. There are others, too, like: Bugs Bunny, Alvin and the Chipmunks, Winnie the Pooh and Scooby Doo. The list goes on and on—cartoon animals with human characteristics and personalities. It's no wonder we treat our pets like human beings.

---

[10] Agnes Norfleet, "Christian Pets," *The Presbyterian Outlook*, 2009.

When I was in college, I took in a dog that I'd found, who'd been hurt. He lived with me a while in my dorm room. During the day, he'd trot around campus, and sometimes sit outside my English class listening to the poetry of Wordsworth and Keats. On weekend nights he'd often go to fraternity parties—sometimes overdoing it a bit. He even appeared on stage once at a Parents' Day Program. When I got a call from the people in charge of housing telling me I needed to get him out, I argued that he was cleaner and better behaved than most of the guys in the dorm—which was true.

My home has always been full of animals. The women in my house when I was growing up took in every kind of stray. I once slept tentatively on my back a couple of nights, trying not to disturb a cat on my stomach who was recuperating from hip surgery. My mother often shooed bugs out the door rather than stepping on them. "They're God's creatures, Sugar," she said. Of course, we carried on conversations with our pets. Our animals were always full of insights. There was one story my grandmother told about her mother, Kate, changing her parrot's cage. The bird slipped out and a hawk quickly swept down. As the parrot was carried away into the sky, it cried out: "Look, Kate, I'm flying." I'm sure it was a traumatic experience—whatever really happened.

We bond closely to certain animals. So, it's no wonder that, as a parent, we've likely known a time when our child turned to us and asked: "Daddy, Mommy, is Spot in heaven?" I suspect few of us would say, "No" in that instance, even if we weren't at all sure about the theology of it. Children ask the hardest questions, often which still roll around somewhere in our minds, and which we've never really been able to answer satisfactorily. A friend of mine was struggling with her session's policy on the burial of pets in the church memorial garden and had ventured into the subject of animal salvation with a colleague. The colleague told her of being called to the deathbed of one of his church members, a former U.S.

Congressman. The man's one question, as he lay dying, was, "Would his dog go to heaven?" The pastor, without missing a beat, said, "Absolutely." [11]

It was purely a pastoral response. But what is our theology regarding the salvation of pets? What does the Bible have to say? It might seem a rather silly subject to some, but I believe it has important implications for how we live in this world. Not long ago, there was a debate posted on the internet that had made the rounds. The debate supposedly was going on between two churches who were posting short, rather terse responses to each other on their church signs. The gist of it was that one church started by posting: "All Dogs Go to Heaven." The other countered by saying: "Only humans go to heaven, read your Bible." The first said next: "God loves all creatures, dogs included." The other said: "Dogs don't have souls; this is not open for debate." And so forth. It turns out the debate wasn't really going on between any two real churches, but it was amazing how many people were interested in the subject and logging on to the site.

When Uga (the University of Georgia mascot) died this year, local radio sports talk shows were inundated with calls from people about it—many grieving. A cartoon in the Atlanta paper (Luckovich, AJC) showed Saint Peter welcoming Uga through the Pearly Gates by way of a doggie door. Will Rogers once quipped that if there are no dogs in heaven then when he died, he wanted to go where they went. There is a society of atheists, who apparently advertise that since they'll be left behind after the Rapture, they'll be glad to arrange for daily care of the pets of some of the rest of us—for a pre-arranged fee.

---

[11] Ibid.

I have to say, I've done funerals of sorts for my dogs, cats, even rabbits and hamsters. There have been prayers offered, and appeal for God to take care of them—and this not just for the sake of the children either. There often have been some jokes, but also tears—not unlike a lot of human funerals I've done. My experience in this, though, has been well limited to fuzzy, warm-blooded animals—except maybe a goldfish or two. Fred, the black snake, who lives under my house, taking care of the mice, I have a lot of respect for, but I'll probably never do a service for him. But, I'm not sure God bases Fred's salvation on the same criteria. Surely, God loves all the creatures.

The Bible, of course, mentions lots of animals: from ants and locusts to monsters of the sea. There are more dogs mentioned than cats, but not necessarily in a good light. Sheep, the animals living most closely with people then, probably got the best reviews. There are all kinds of life lessons, spiritual lessons in the Bible, drawn from animals. And there are a few like the great fish that swallows Jonah, who are instrumental in God's purposes. In the beginning, Genesis tells us, God breathed into them, too, to give life, and all creation was pronounced good. Genesis tells us that when human beings fell in sin, all creation fell with us. It wasn't their fault, but the animals and all creatures have suffered right along with us and because of us. The Noah story tells us that God saved only one human family, but that all animal species were important for the good of the world. Biologists will tell you the same thing: every creature has its place in the community, (though I'm not so sure about chiggers).

Animals certainly have been important for things like sniffing out bombs and people buried in rubble (like recently in Haiti). Some dogs can even detect bladder cancer in humans. But pets also have offered something more spiritual, through their companionship for people in nursing homes and physical and spiritual therapy for disabled children. Just ask Cy about the horses at Calvin Center. The

Noah story echoed again in the words of the prophet, Hosea, makes clear that God's covenant after the flood is with all living creatures (Hosea 2 and 4). Our part, certainly, is to care for them and guide them. Social deviants are often detected first by their cruel treatment of animals. We have a holy responsibility as stewards, caretakers of creation.

Still, Jesus ate lamb and fish, and I do, too. And if there's ever a choice between the safety of my 7-year-old grandson and my 17-year-old dog, it's the dog who's going to have to suffer. When my vet told me a $5,000 cataract operation would save the sight of my previous old and beloved dog, I asked how much longer she really could go on. I hope I wouldn't have done that with my mother.

Jesus told of the Father's love for the birds of the air, but also said that God loves us even more. Catholics, Episcopalians, Lutherans and even a few Presbyterians have services of blessing animals. It's been done in the National Cathedral. The prayer often used is the one we prayed at the beginning of the service today. The part left out was: "God, we ask you to bless this pet. By the power of your love, enable it to live according to your plan." I confess, I bless my old dog every morning as I leave her. And she has blessed me in many ways.

There's an interesting line in the Jonah story, at the very end where God says to Jonah, after God has saved Nineveh: "And should I not pity Nineveh, that great city in which there are more than one hundred twenty thousand persons who do not know their right hand from their left, and also much cattle?" There are places in the Psalms which speak of animals praising God. Some people will say that only refers to their life here and now. Maybe that's what Psalm 36 means when it says: ".... humans and beasts, you save, O God." But there are other texts—texts like the Romans text we read, which speaks of the whole creation groaning for the hope of redemption. The new heaven and new earth are basic to our Reformed understanding. Calvin, Luther and Wesley affirmed as much. There is a passage in Revelation which speaks of animals around the throne of God. But who can make sense of Revelation?

None of us knows the particulars of heaven. The Bible is mighty skimpy on those—asking us rather to trust in the grace and love of God. Surely, if we love animals, God loves them even more. The image of God, I believe is found to a lesser degree in animals than humans. But sometimes I think of the story of Balaam's ass, who sees the heavenly messenger when the prophet cannot. And I'm reminded of the old, blind dachshund I had to chain to a clothesline, so she wouldn't wander into trouble. Late one day, as the sun was setting, I saw her sitting, looking out toward the heavens, a rabbit sitting beside her, looking in the same direction. And I think again of Balaam's ass, and of the picture Isaiah gives of the Kingdom of Heaven—where the wolf sits down with the lamb. Maybe heaven is not complete without them. Maybe some of them are pointing us the way.

From Childhood
2 Timothy 3:14-15

Officially in the life of the Church, at least in many churches, today is the seventh and last Sunday of Easter. Of course, everybody knows it's Mother's Day. Even my official Presbyterian Planning Calendar notes that. In this congregation we've had a tradition we've called Senior Sunday- which doesn't refer to senior citizens, but rather to graduating high school seniors. At times the themes of Mother's Day and Senior Sunday for us have been conflated, which has seemed an appropriate time to think about parents and children.

Some years we've had a good-sized group of high school seniors, while other years we've had only a few. This is a year in which we have only a few. So, I am focusing today not just on graduating high school seniors, but on all the young people of the church and all who are mothers, or grandmothers, or aunts of these young people, and on anybody else who might believe we have some responsibility for the Christian life and nurture of our young people.

I find myself repeating things more these days. I know it's common as we get older. My grandmother repeated things often, especially stories. We, grandchildren, got to where we knew the lines, by heart. And I am grateful. As I said before, I think, sometimes maybe that is God's way of making sure we remember. We must be told some things over and over for them to stick with us.

Advertisers know this very well. We are bombarded by the same ad over and over. We hear the same jingle again and again until we wake up with it playing in our heads: "Nationwide is on our side"; "Five-dollar, five-dollar footlong"; "Why don't you just meet me in the middle." Yes, see how you can sing along with me. We can't get them out of our heads.

There are songs, hymns, responses I hear on Sunday mornings in worship that also stick in my brain. "There's an endless song echoes in my soul," the choir sang today. It's said that we probably get more of our theology from our hymns than from anywhere else. Which is why I try to choose them carefully each week. My choices aren't always the ones you might choose. People complain sometimes about not singing some of "the old hymns" - even if I point out that they might go back to the 1500s. We have various favorites among the congregation because many of us have grown up in different traditions.

I'm grateful for some of the songs that I learned as a child in Sunday school and worship: "Jesus loves me, this I know, for the Bible tells me so"; "Red and yellow, black and white, they are precious in his sight; Jesus loves the little children of the world." They are songs that have found a place in my memory, and I believe have molded my faith and life more deeply than I once knew.

At the beginning of this letter of Paul's he gives thanks for the faith of the young man, Timothy, a faith nurtured by Timothy's mother Eunice and grandmother Lois. Faith isn't inherited, of course; we must make our own decisions; we must discern what is truth and how we're called to live. There are so many voices out there telling us who we are and what we should want and what we deserve; voices telling us how we should look and dress, and what will make us happy; all these things that keep playing in our heads. What we hope, as parents and family, as church family, is that the Word of God, the Good News of the Gospel, will be repeated to us over and over as we grow up into the people God calls us to be.

You young people, your mothers and fathers knew they couldn't do all this on their own. So, they found a community where others stood with them and made holy vows to help them. They found a community that promised to pray for you and for them, to pick you up when you fell, to tell you the stories of Jesus, to remind you that no matter how far you wandered, you had been claimed by the One who truly is your keeper through all things and from whose love you can never be separated.

Your parents want to give you so many things, and there are so many opportunities available to you, so many things to take up your time and energy and shape your thoughts and your understanding of life. Your parents run themselves ragged trying to give you those opportunities. But, when they brought you to be baptized, when they brought you into this community of faith, they did it because, as hopeful as they might have been for your intellectual prowess or your athletic achievement- even as hard as they might pray for your physical safety- above all else, they hoped for your heart to be open to the grace of God.

Oh, I know. There were times when I was young my parents had to drag me into church. Yeah, it's true. I thought the service was soooo long, and the preacher wasn't ever going to stop. But, somehow, something kept seeping into my mind, even when I was sleeping, kept creeping into my heart, even if I thought I wasn't listening.

Jesus told a story about a sower, a farmer, throwing out seed. It kept landing on hard ground, rocky soil, or amid briars. But, he kept throwing it out. And you know what? Some of it still took root and grew. In fact, it grew into an amazing harvest. I believe God is persistent like that too. God uses all of us, not just preachers and youth leaders, but also those of us teaching Sunday school and singing the Word in the choir, and parents and others who have made those vows for the children of the church. God calls all of us to keep throwing it out there, the Word, the Good News, with the promise that God can do more than we could ever imagine.

Paul tells Timothy, "Continue in what you've learned and firmly believed, knowing from whom you learned it." Look around you. It's from these people and through these people you have been learning about grace and faith, about the love of God in Jesus Christ. You know, there are a lot of wild and crazy sounding things in the Bible. There are people who profess to believe some things other people just find foolish. Which leads them to take some stands others won't take, to stretch their love beyond the limits of where many people won't go. Despite how some situations look, they trust the One who claims that love is stronger than hate, that life is stronger than death, that the only thing worth giving your life to is the One who has given life to you.

Mr. Dan keeps telling you you're not just the future of the Church; you are the Church now. We've been so proud of you who have stood up here and read the Scriptures and preached the sermons; who've led us with song and music and prayers; who've helped lead Vacation Bible School; who've taken to the streets to walk for justice and compassion; who've handed out food to the hungry; who've drawn bulletin covers at Advent and Lent; some of you who as very young children have drawn pictures for me over the years, and written me notes of faith and encouragement that cover the shelves in my study. Like the one written to me after I preached on Jesus telling the Palm Sunday crowd that if they didn't shout out his welcome, the very stones would cry out. And you told me: "Rock on, Mr. Billy. Rock on!" Thank you.

We know some of you are graduating; others are moving on. We'll miss you. But, we've been trying to help prepare you for this time. We've been blessed to have you in our midst, and we will continue to hold up you and your parents in our prayers. We made promises to God.

Faith is a journey, a life-long journey. You're not done. So, I tell you again, as Paul says: "Continue in what you have learned and firmly believed, knowing from whom you learned it, and how from childhood you have known the sacred writings that are able to instruct you for salvation for faith in Christ Jesus."

In Lieu of Advice

Luke 15:1-3a; 11-32

Graduation Sunday

Often, when Jesus wanted to get something across, he didn't give advice, he told stories. And there is no story better remembered than this one. For those of you having recently graduated and now going off, in some sense, to make your way in the world, there is a lot of advice we'd like to give you (we, your parents, elders, leaders, members of the body of Christ in this place). But, maybe, what's better is a story.

The fact is, in some ways, this story almost seems to run counter to the advice we'd like to give. For instance, that part about the father holding out his son's inheritance and saying, "Here, take what you want." You're not likely to hear that from your fathers. I know your fathers. And truthfully, what parents would so readily give up control of what they had worked so hard to accumulate, just to place it in the hands of their children to do whatever they wanted to do with it? The father's not dead yet, for goodness sake! No, most fathers I know would say something like: "Well, I'll give you enough to get started. Let's see what you can do with it. You need to learn something about hard work and responsibility. So, spend it wisely; invest some; save some. These are not easy times, you know."

No matter how much you're taking with you as you leave, just the leaving itself brings up a mixture of emotions. For you, there might or might not be all the excitement with which the younger son here leaves home. I do remember some excitement when I got the chance. But most of us have had some anxiety about it, too. Will I be able to make it after all? Do I really want to make all these decisions for myself? How much will I really miss family and friends once the break is made?

For parents, it's also a mixed bag. There are moments every parent has thought: It's time. You need to get out of the house. We need for you to get out of the house. And yet, there will be an emptiness. And what their heart will long for more than almost anything else in this world, is to see you coming back through the door, empty-handed, or even with a load of dirty laundry.

One of the most difficult things for any parent is to let you go on your own. It was hard to let loose of you when you took your first steps, to let loose the bicycle when you first rode off, to turn loose the steering wheel when you first drove away. It is very difficult for parents to risk letting you make your own mistakes. That old saying that, "This is going to hurt me more than it's going to hurt you," is mostly true for parents. We've known from the moment the doctor first put you in our arms that love is the most wonderful thing in life, but also the hardest.

There are things in this world that look very attractive. Goodness knows, we are bombarded daily with what the world offers up as the good life. But, it's not the truth. The very reason your parents brought you through the doors of a church and asked the minister to pour the waters of baptism over you is so that you would know the truth. They realized that whatever they could do by themselves would not be enough- it would never be enough. They knew that at times they would fail you. What they needed was a new community of people who would pray for you and tell you of the love of God- a love greater and deeper even than their love of you. What they would be praying for you above all else is that like the younger son, you would, at some point, in some way, "come to yourself" – that you would wake up to the truth.

Not that it would ever happen all at once. It's not that the young man has arrived at the truth when he first gets up out of the pig pit and heads home. In fact, when the father sees him, he's still "a long way off," which means more than physical distance. He is just beginning to sort some things out. But, the father, who's been watching the horizon ever since he left, hikes up his robe, throwing dignity to the wind, and runs out to meet him. Before the son can begin his spiel about how sorry he is and how he'll be glad just to work as a servant, because he certainly doesn't deserve anything more, the father grabs him up in his arms, calling to all that will hear: "This is my son!"

Not all of us are parents or will be. But all of us are children. We are children who, like the prodigal, have made mistakes, experienced failures, ventured into a far country in one way or another. But, you see, this is not about our faith in God, but God's faith in us. God waits for any moment, any crack in our defenses, any point of desperation, for some inkling of divine love to filter through, so that we start back toward him, to be received into his open arms. We can never go so far that we are no longer a child of God. We might go far enough that we forget it, but God doesn't forget. God's love knows no bounds. As the Apostle Paul says, nothing – not the highest highs or the lowest lows, no power on this earth or beyond – can separate us from the love of God in Jesus Christ our Lord (Romans 8: 38-39).

Make no mistake, it's not about our deserving – which makes this sometimes a difficult story for us who are so often used to giving or receiving good advice and thinking we really do earn our way. It's not even about our remorse, or our determination to do better. It's about God's surprising love. This is not about one brother coming back to be like the other: responsible, hardworking, loyal. For, you see, the elder brother is even a harder case. In a sense, he's a long way off, too; because he thinks that there are things he deserves in life, things he's earned by following all the rules. But, it's not so much about the rules as about the heart. The truth is, life itself is a gift, and a grateful heart is what it means to live by grace – the only way to experience a truly abundant life. The older brother hears the music, but he's not caught up in the rhythm; he's not able to dance.

When we first moved to Covington, Graham was 6 years old. (I can tell this story because it was a long time ago and because he's not here). He'd had a difficult time. We moved him in the middle of the first grade. He missed his friends, and the school he had just adjusted to at such an important time in his life. And he was a sad little fellow, moping around. He was in a far country. He was mad at us some and we kept trying to draw him into things. The church had a retreat to Camp Calvin. Most of the church went – I suppose to scope out the new minister and family. It was a wonderful time of fellowship and warmth. And at one point, we were all lined up in chairs for a program. Graham was sitting near the front with some new friends who had welcomed him into their group. Some music started playing, and Graham jumped up and started dancing. And I knew he was home.

In lieu of advice, what we hope and pray for you who have graduated is that in this community of faith you have known something of the love of God – the God who offers you your true inheritance, and blesses you on your way; the God who redeems your life from the pits, and receives you always with open arms.

Remembered

Deuteronomy 26:1-11

"Holiday" means "holy day," a concept left over from a time when many people in our society lived their lives according to a religious calendar rather than three-day weekends. It comes from a time when Church festivals, for Christians, were the most popular things going.

Following the seasons of the Church year, and celebrating the holy days, is a way in which we remember who we are and to whom we belong in the midst of a culture that has largely forgotten. In an important way, that is what Sundays are for us each week.

Today is Trinity Sunday on the Church Calendar, a day for celebrating the One who is the Father, Son and Holy Spirit, the Creator, Redeemer and Sustainer, the One God whom we experience in different ways. Sometimes the Church's high holy days converge with days that in some ways the culture around us still remembers, and in some sense still marks as holy.

I find myself repeating things more often these days. Remembering is not always easy, even when we are not that old. We are busy people. Our mental mailboxes get crowded. Most of us resort to all kinds of methods to help us remember. We have calendars on our desks or in our devices. Some of us place sticky notes in strategic places. I find the refrigerator door a good place since I visit it regularly. I ask people who tell me things at the door after worship to hand me a note, or to leave a message on my phone, or better yet, to tell Peni in the church office.

I worry a lot that I'm going to forget something important. I read a story once about a pastor who forgot he had a wedding that day. I have nightmares about that kind of thing. T.S. Eliot has that memorable line about modern life, that we are "distracted from distraction by distraction." [12] We forget what's important, what life is about. Earlier in the Book of Deuteronomy, God tells the people to post God's teachings on their hands, and between their eyes, and on their doorposts, so they won't forget them.

There is a lot of forgetting and remembering in the Bible. Have you noticed? Pharaoh's chief butler, after he was released from prison, forgot Joseph and how Joseph had helped him while they were in prison together. But later he remembered Joseph and helped him to be released from prison. Many years later, another Pharaoh forgot Joseph, at least forgot how much Joseph and his family had contributed to the welfare and economy of Egypt and grew fearful of the rising number of these foreigners in their midst.

There are several places in the scriptures where we're told that the people forgot God; forgot what God had done for them; forgot their history; forgot that they were God's people. That's why the people are reminded-again- in the passage we've just read this morning, and why heads of families have continued to tell this story to their children and their children's children, lest they forget, lest they forget. "A wandering Aramean was my father" - and your father. The story is ours. We are that people the story teller says. Remember, since you have come into this land, the peace you have enjoyed, the abundance of this land flowing with milk and honey. Remember that you did not win it by your own efforts. It is the gift of God.

Remembering, in the Bible, is more than just being reminded of something that has slipped our mind. It is the bringing to mind a fuller and deeper awareness of what has happened to make us who we are and who we can yet be. It is meant to move us ahead in the right path. There are some things in our past we'd like to forget;

---

[12] T. S. Eliot, *Burnt Norton*, 1936.

there are some things sometimes so painful, our minds won't let us remember. There are times in Scripture, where we're told that even God forgets. Our sins, for instance- and that's a great blessing.

Historians are fond of saying that if you don't know where you've been you can't know where you're heading; that if you don't know your history, you are bound to repeat it. That's why African-Americans keep going out and marching over the Edmund Pettus Bridge in Selma every so often. And why there are Holocaust museums. It's why old men and women return to the beaches at Normandy and to the Vietnam Memorial wall in Washington. It's to pay tribute and to grieve, but also to enable people to move forward. At our best, we seek to learn from the past, so that we can participate in the hope of a better day.

Memorial Day, it seems to me, is one of those rare days still consecrated by our society, that comes, or can come, very close to what we hold to as Christians: a day to grieve over loss; a day to acknowledge evil and our part in it; a day to honor sacrifices made and be grateful; a day to pray for and work toward the peace that has defied our understanding; a day to give thanks for the bounty of this land and the God who has blessed us beyond our deserving; a day to pray for God to free us from the past and lead us toward the future God has promised for us.

There's a wonderful line in that familiar passage in John's gospel (John 14), where Jesus has been telling his anxious and fearful disciples that soon he will be leaving them. But, he tells them, "I am going to prepare a place for you." In the meantime, he says, the Father will be sending you the Holy Spirit who will guide you and "bring to your remembrance all that I have said to you." The Holy Spirit as the Great Reminder.

Often, we forget, believing that we've been left alone, left to our own devices. "How long, O Lord? Will you forget me forever?" the psalmist cries (Psalm 13). Our timing is not always God's timing; maybe because God must work so hard to work through us, to work despite us. But, again and again, we are reminded of how God does not forget us. When we are baptized, our names are called out and we are promised that no matter who else forgets us, even though we might forget who we are in one way or another, God never forgets us. God's claim on us is forever.

Preacher and author, Barbara Brown Taylor, tells of spending a week at a monastery. Every morning, every noon, every evening and night, guests are invited to join the brothers in the chapel, a room with a whole wall of windows opening toward the sea. At the daily Eucharist, the same monks who washed the dishes wearing bib aprons, show up in floor-length vestments to serve communion. During the week she was there, the prayers of the people included the names of those who'd died each day in Iraq, along with those who had died of cancer, or old age, or whatever. She says, "They were named in the presence of God's people, who make it our business to note even the fall of a sparrow, trusting that our lives are bound up with all other lives in Christ." [13]

There are some of you who have come back from dangerous places, far away. And we give thanks. There are others of you who grieve the loss of those close to you who did not come back. Sometimes, going about all the things we are busy with in our lives, we forget. We forget there are still wars being fought. We forget there are well over a million U. S. soldiers in about 150 countries around the world. Those who have family members in those places never forget.

---

[13] Barbara Brown Taylor, "Naming the Dead," *The Christian Century*, July 1, 2007.

On this day, we call out the names of those people from among us: David and Savannah Cannon Rickert, Mike Laib, John Rossi. Among the names of others for whom we pray this morning, we pray for their protection, giving thanks to the One who always remembers their names and the names of all God's children. We pray to the One who promises never to leave them- or any of us- alone; the One who promises never to leave us finally to our own devices. We pray in the name of the Father, the Son and the Holy Spirit.

Freedom
Exodus 6:1-13; Luke 4:16-21

Observing the seasons of the Church Year is meant to remind us to whom our lives belong. If we are faithful, our lives will move to a different rhythm than that to which many around us move. Still there is no doubt that we're not only aware of, but celebrants of several occasions which mark the civil calendar: New Year's, Labor Day, Memorial Day, Father's Day, Mother's Day. Sometimes such occasions do provide us with an opportunity to listen for God's word and to consider how our faith just might speak to issues raised by the celebration of these occasions.

The texts this morning are not ones prescribed by the Church lectionary, but rather ones I've chosen for us to listen for God's Word as we draw near to our country's Independence Day celebration. The first scripture comes from the Book of Exodus. It recalls the central event of the Old Testament: the deliverance of God's people from slavery in Egypt. This text presents Moses during his wrangling with Pharaoh. Moses is completely frustrated by the lack of results he's getting and the fact that all he's been able to do is to make Israel's burdens heavier, as Pharaoh has tightened his grip... "Lord, I told you so." And the people have become so disheartened because they know Pharaoh's power and cannot believe the promises of God.

Listen: Exodus 6:1-13.

The second text comes from Luke's gospel. It's Jesus' first sermon, in his hometown, when he has just come back from being tempted by Satan in the wilderness where he'd gone after his baptism by John. What he is given is the lectionary text for the day- a reading from the prophet Isaiah. It outlines Jesus' mission and ministry- what already is happening through him in their presence.

Listen: Luke 4:16-21.

What is it you think of when you think of the Fourth of July? For years, when my children were little, we got together over in the Fairfield neighborhood. The area had once been Donald Stephenson's farm, but all that was left of the farm was a silo next to the neighborhood swimming pool. There were by then several members of this church who lived in the neighborhood- with lots of young children. Together with others who lived there, we had a grand parade each year. The children and Donald, well into his senior years, decorated their bicycles with red, white, and blue streamers and flags. Smaller children, with the help of parents, decorated their tricycles or Hot Wheels. Some parents of the littlest ones decorated their baby carriages. And when Miss Katie, Donald's wife, gave the signal, we launched the parade down the street. It wasn't a very long street, so usually when we finished, we'd all turn around and start again. Then, we'd have a picnic by the pool.

In more recent years, my family often has been at the beach on the Fourth of July. There we gather with a group of old friends whose children are grown and beginning to have their own. We gather for a meal. But, before we eat, there is always a raising of the flag and one of the old Navy guys (not the store), leads us in the Pledge of Allegiance and singing of "America the Beautiful" or "The Star-Spangled Banner." Then, they turn to me to pray- which is always some recitation of our gratitude for our blessings: country, home, friends, family- blessings which seem so very evident as we stand there and which I have a hard time getting through without choking up.

If you asked most people what it is primarily we celebrate on the Fourth of July, I have no doubt that the overwhelming response would be "freedom." America is "the land of the free and the home of the brave," a land where people have come seeking freedom and laid down their lives to preserve it. We have freedom to gather when and where we want, freedom to speak our mind, freedom to live as we choose, and freedom to worship as we believe. People have continued through the years, to line up to get here- just as our own immigrant ancestors did. Our ideals, those on which this country was founded, have been greater than what we've usually been able to live out, and deeper than the meaning we've often perceived. When we've championed freedom for "all people," we've time and again left some out: women, people of dark skin, those of different sexual orientations. But, those on the outside have reminded us of what we've professed.

The God we know in scripture is a God who offers us freedom. From the very beginning, we have been given choices (way back to Genesis) - to choose this God, or not. A God who nevertheless keeps seeking us, no matter how far we wander, who keeps responding to our cries when we recognize our true needs. People suffering from oppression have always found in the Bible a God who acts to set them free. God tells Moses: "I have heard the groaning of the people of Israel whom the Egyptians hold in bondage and I have remembered my covenant." Jesus reads the words of the prophet Isaiah: "The spirit of the Lord is upon me. The spirit of God has sent me to proclaim release to the captives... to set at liberty those who are oppressed." It's the reason he was crucified. He is the Truth as he is the Way and the Life that sets us free.

I have to say though, that I'm often disturbed with so much of the popular conception of freedom: freedom to do as I want, no matter how it affects others; freedom to pursue my happiness without regard for the welfare of others; the idea of freedom which carries no responsibility; which draws tight, close borders around me and mine. When we were in New Orleans some years ago helping to clean up after hurricane Katrina, living in a tent city behind the First Union Presbyterian Church with about 100 folks from Presbyterian churches all over the country, there was a young guy- a teenager with spiked hair of various colors, some piercings and wearing a nice collection of in-your-face t-shirts. He carried a guitar over his shoulder and once when playing for vespers, announced himself to be an atheist anarchist. I was never sure what he meant by it exactly. As you well know, Christians don't believe in atheists. But, he seemed to believe in having no government, no church (at least not the institutional church) and no God- at least not the kind we often think of. But, evidently, he did see the need for some sort of community- a community of nurture and care for one another- one that would reach out to include different kinds of folks and help people in need. In some very important ways, I thought, "This kid is getting it right." Oh, sure, he had a ways to go-but it's a journey for us all. And for many of us, the journey has been long and winding.

When God set the children of Israel free from Egypt, they spent forty years wandering in the desert. It wasn't that they didn't know the way to the Promised Land- like they needed a map or something. It was more that they didn't know how to get there because they didn't know how to live as free people. They didn't know that to be truly free was to recognize their dependence on God and one another. The Apostle Paul, speaking of freedom, says it is not so much freedom "from" as freedom "for." We have been set free from bondage to sin and the threat of death, set free from concern only for ourselves, to live gratefully, in service to God. Now that sounds ironic: like exchanging one set of chains for another. But, that is the only way we will know the truly abundant life, the joy which we are offered. To be left alone, in fact, is hell itself.

There is always a revolutionary nature to the kind of freedom God invites us into. It always in some ways challenges the structures, the powers that be, the might which makes right, the money which makes the rules. It gives voice to the least likely: those like Jeremiah who think they're too young; or like Moses who think they don't have the power; or like those who have ascended from humble roots to the highest office in the land. Freedom, Jesus says, is good news to the poor - not grabbing for all we can get. It continually calls us into a new kind of community where outsiders become insiders and the last become the first for a change. It is where we trust the One we profess to believe in and try to live by the methods this One prescribes, rather than our own devices.

The Apostle Paul taught the slave Onesimus that we can be free even when we are in bondage. He taught this from his own jail cell. But, in his Letter to Philemon, Onesimus' owner, he told Philemon to receive his slave back as a Christian brother, the child of his true owner. Any real application of that principle cannot help but challenge the very system. Martin Luther King, Jr. heard that in the scriptures, and writing from a jail cell in Birmingham, he spoke of how none can be free unless all are free; and that if we are people of faith, then we must act- and act according to the methods of the One who makes the demands. He said: "We will win our freedom because the sacred heritage of our nation and the eternal will of God are embodied in our echoing demands." [14] There are voices that still remind us of those things.

There are those who believe we are a chosen nation, that God has a special covenant with us. Well, the scriptures speak of God's covenant with Israel and what it means to be chosen by God. Israel was chosen not for privilege, but for service. Through them, God would bless all nations. But, continually they kept drawing their

---

[14] Martin Luther King, Jr., "Letter from a Birmingham Jail."

borders closer, seeing themselves only as God's people, God's favorite ones. The prophets kept preaching and they kept running them off. And Jesus kept stepping over the lines and you know what they did to him.

In an interview sometime back, Billy Graham spoke about how his life and ministry had changed. He said: "It was a mistake to identify the kingdom of God with the American way of life.... I've come to see that other cultures have their own way that may be of just as great a value. I think we consume too much and think we have become too materialistic. I spend half my time abroad now. I feel that God has called me to a world ministry. I don't look upon myself as an ambassador of the U.S., as I did at one time. I look upon myself as a world ambassador." [15]

I would challenge anybody that I love my country, my region, my town, my family, my church, as much as anybody anywhere. I am truly blessed. But, I cannot get away from the Biblical command to stretch my borders, to proclaim far and wide the Truth that sets us free, the great Good News, to love more and more the world God has so loved (John 3:16).

If this nation is chosen, it is surely to be a blessing to all nations. If it is influenced by the faith to which Jesus calls us – it is foremost in its compassion and it's stand for justice. In this sanctuary, there are no foreigners. Here we are all only children of God. The symbol in this place, above all, is the cross of the Christ, who laid down his life for all. There should be no confusion about whom we serve first, and who gives us our marching orders. We shall have no other gods- not country, or home, or family.

---

[15] Billy Graham, quoted in "America Is Not God's Only Kingdom," *Parade Magazine*, Feb. 1, 1981, p.6.

The Christian Church doesn't exist because of America. It was around long before. It exists by the grace of God. It is only God who gives us the freedom to worship- only God. Some of the truest worship is in lands that are not free, where people worship still under threat of persecution and death. We are called to live into the freedom we're given. It will always require us to give our lives completely- not always to die, but to live sacrificially, standing for justice, working for peace, proclaiming release to the captives. If we can in any way be a light to the nations, it is only by reflecting the One who is the Light.

Bearing and Following the Word into the World

Luke 10:25-28; Romans 12:9-21

Sometimes when I get toward the end or even the middle of a sermon series, I start to wish maybe I'd thought a little more about some of the latter sermons and where they might lead us. But by then, I'm stuck. Sometimes things happen in the world, or in the community, or in the church that can't be ignored, even if I'd rather ignore them.

This is the fourth in the series on "Worship," following our order in the bulletin. The first week we focused on "Gathering Around the Word," on how God woos us into worship, then breaks into our routine lives with the Good News of life to which God calls us. The second week, we considered the "Proclaiming of the Word," how we listen together to hear the Word of God in scripture, most clearly in the Christ we meet in Scripture. And last week, we thought about "Responding to the Word," how we are to be "doers and not hearers only."

Today, it seems timely, that we come to "Bearing and Following the Word into the World." Some churches have a sign over the door as people go out, which says: "You are entering the mission field." The texts this morning come from Jesus' words recorded in Luke's gospel, and Paul's words from his Letter to the church in Rome. The text from Luke includes some of the most familiar words of Jesus, as he speaks with one who is an "expert" on the scriptures. As he often does, Jesus answers a question with a question. Like last week's text from Micah where the prophet says: "You know what is good and what the Lord requires of you (you *know*): to do justice, to love kindness and to walk humbly with God; here, Jesus asks the man: "What does the scripture say? How do you read it?"

He might well have wished he'd left it at that, but the man goes on: "So, who is my neighbor?" What follows, of course, is one of Jesus' most remembered parables, that of the Good Samaritan. Like all of Jesus' parables, we either walk away shaking our heads, or we feel slapped in the face, thinking, "Thanks, I needed that." What Jesus does here is to lead us beyond our narrow definition of "neighbor," to stretch the limits of what we call love. The surprise is not so much the way the "good people" act, as it is the way the one acts whom we least expect to be our neighbor, the one we expect to be most hostile toward us, the one of whom we are afraid. Jesus holds up the Samaritan as a model. It doesn't sit well.

The second text comes from Paul's words to the Church in Rome. He speaks of "genuine love." When I talk with couples getting married, I remind them of Paul's words here and elsewhere that present love not just as feeling, but as the actions we take even when we're not feeling so loving, when the other seems not so loveable.

Controversy can find us. I've been quoted and pictured in the *Atlanta Journal/Constitution* this week. They called me; I didn't call them. But, as I've told some folks, I'm glad they still want any input from a Christian minister. Obviously, somebody pointed them in my direction. I always shudder to think what might be printed in a soundbite. But I do believe God calls Christians to speak out on things. I don't presume to speak for the whole church. Our church has people of many different opinions on many different subjects. I believe that tends to be good for us. I never press the session to make a statement on behalf of the whole church, and I've been grateful for people who do hang in there with one another when things are not decided their way. I've tried to follow their faithful example in that.

I tell you a story, and like all stories, you'll have to find your own place in it. I was invited on Tuesday to go visit the Imam and his Muslim community in Doraville. I don't know how I got the invitation. It was a small group –nine of us- men and women, some I knew and some I didn't, from different sides of the "political aisle"; several pastors of local churches, black and white. There was no shared agenda, no plans before going. We arrived at a couple of small buildings, old but nicely kept, in a neighborhood, though there was a business to one side of them with which they shared their parking lot. There was a fence in the back, by the basketball goal, but people evidently walk through all the time on their way to Home Depot. We were warmly greeted by children giving each of us a bouquet of red, white and blue flowers.

They welcomed us into a small room filled with children in their traditional garb and teenagers and young adults in jeans and t-shirts with brand logos and college insignias. There were a few old guys (at least my age) from this community. We sat with one another and talked, asking questions of one another, until they served us lunch and we broke bread together. After a while, the men moved into their worship area, a small room about half the size of our fellowship hall, where we had a group discussion. No questions were off limits. You can see part of that discussion on video on the *Atlanta Journal/Constitution* website. There were a couple of *Atlanta Journal/Constitution* reporters there.

The community has a small school for children through high school years. Then most of them go off to college: Georgia Tech, Georgia State, UGA and other places. The Imam told of his desire for his community to find a larger place, an affordable piece of land, where they could have their own cemetery and burial preparation facility, along with a new mosque and maybe eventually a small neighborhood of houses. They don't have much money. He said plans would develop over several years, he hoped. He spoke, choking back tears a couple of times, of his desire to be a good neighbor, to open part of the land for a community park, even perhaps to offer to sell a piece of the land to a Christian church. He said it's more land than they need. He spoke of his love for America and why he came to this country years ago. Many in the community were born here; others have lived in the area as citizens for decades.

All of us were overwhelmed by their kindness and gentleness, their hospitality. I was reminded of the hospitality of some Muslim families with whom I visited in the Middle East. The Imam said he'd love to have others come visit, and I know some who are making those plans. Except during prayer times their doors are always open – unlike the doors at our church.

I do know that a Muslim representative – not from that community- is coming here soon to talk with any people who have questions about their religion. He does this in many places. He told me, if many of the things said about them in our community meetings were true, he'd be scared too. Ironically, the Imam wanted to come, but he was advised by some folks here not to come because he might be in danger. It's very telling, that those who spoke in the court house meeting here in favor of welcoming them were, a young Jewish woman, a Catholic woman, a black woman who'd had crosses burned in her yard, and a Muslim guy who'd lived a good while here and never had any problem with his neighbors.

Regarding this situation, as a citizen of this country, I believe we need to be vigilant regarding the rights of all citizens. We cannot expect our right to worship to be protected if that is not the case for others. It's in the very first Amendment of the Constitution. It's basic. Despite what some of us might want, the landscape is changing and will continue to change, whether these people come at this time or not.

What concerns me even more is what I hear Jesus saying. I admit that I find Jesus naïve at times: The last shall be first, the first last; if somebody demands you go with them a mile, go with them two; turn the other cheek; deny yourself; love your enemies and pray for those who persecute you. Does he really understand the world we live in today? Sometimes I wish Jesus would just be quiet. But, I've committed my life to trusting him; and sometimes I follow through.

Jesus said we're to love our neighbors as ourselves. He didn't say which neighbors or that we could choose just the ones that we like and are easy to get along with. He said, if you love only those who love you, what reward is that? (Matthew 5: 46-48) He did not say love is easy or safe. But he did say that love is the weapon of choice in the kingdom. It got him killed.

We might not be Jesus, but he called those who would be his disciples to pick up their cross and follow, and I can't just dismiss that lightly as hyperbole. I wish I could find some loopholes in much of what Jesus says, but I can't. Jesus was tempted by the Devil to worship him, to defer to his tactics, same old, same old. But Jesus refused. He wept over the people on his way to the cross, because they still did not know the things that make for peace. I remember reading of some Palestinian Muslims whose mosque had been burned down. Some of their Christian neighbors got together and told them: "We will help you rebuild it." When the Muslims asked why they would do that, they said: "Because we follow Jesus." [16]

---

[16] John M. Buchanan, "Louder than words: Missiological authenticity," *The Christian Century*, February 6, 2017.

Last Sunday morning, I walked into the Foundation Builders Sunday School class where they were engaged in this very conversation. I had no idea what they'd be talking about, but it was very much on their minds, and they wanted to know what others in their church and their preacher thought. It was a room full of folks who said they wanted to keep talking and who, this week, invited a professor from Oxford, Florian Pohl, who teaches Islamic Studies to come and speak to the class.

Few of us know any Muslims or have ever visited a mosque. Oxford College has a number of Muslim students and at least one Muslim professor I know, who are well-loved and held in high regard by many. They are very active in interfaith dialogue and programing. There are several Muslim students who are lab assistants and advisees of people in this congregation who work there, teach there, who are staff and administration and are very concerned about all this. Where do they worship? Is there a chance for us to get to know them better? The Apostle Paul said: "Let love be genuine; hold fast to what is good; practice hospitality; as far as it depends on you, live peaceably with one another."

There is, understandably, some concern for the way some things have been officially handled in this, but there also are people, in our pews, who can speak passionately to not being wanted in their neighborhood and of the flight of those who feared them. There is a risk with love. But, this group seems to offer a chance for us to make some headway. None of us was instrumental in their coming, but what will we do now? Maybe God is inviting us, daring us to risk being "ambassadors of reconciliation," as Paul put it. Maybe our church, our community can be a light – an example to others.

I heard a young man telling his story on the radio. He's not Muslim, but Sikh. Most of us wouldn't know the difference. He wears a turban. He spoke with sadness of how people look at him and avoid him. Some have called him "Osama." He said one of his friends who's not a Sikh, called him to go to lunch. It was a barbeque restaurant. It was in a small town. He was reluctant, but he finally put on his turban and his UGA sweatshirt and went. Entering, he saw and felt the looks of others there. After eating, he got up to go pay. An old woman, she looked 100 he said, came to the cash register. She didn't look up but said, "We don't like your kind here." He thought, oh no, here we go. She looked up and pointed to his sweatshirt. She said, "We're Georgia Tech people here." [17] There is hope.

We leave worship each Sunday with the charge to go out and live as Christ calls us to live. I've heard from many this week, by phone, by e-mail. I've heard from religious leaders and others from this town and county who are coming together; people from far beyond this place, encouraging us, praying for us -watching what we will do. "The word of the cross is foolishness to those who are perishing, but to us who are being saved, it is the power God." We go out from here every Sunday, not only with a charge, but also with a blessing from God Almighty. God is with us and God's Spirit is within us, so that we can do far more than we could ever ask or think.

---

[17] National Public Radio.

Troubled Waters
Mark 4:35-41

Jesus is teaching by the sea. He did that a lot. The mountains slope gently down to the water – like an amphitheater. Jesus is telling stories – teaching parables. So many people have gathered that he is backed up right against the water. So, he steps into a boat and pushes off just a bit. I don't know if he's still teaching by evening, but a crowd is still there.

Sometimes we call this time in the Church year the season of Pentecost and sometimes we call it Ordinary Time. We have our choice. So, some years we hang the red garments of Pentecost and sometimes the green of Ordinary Time. Ordinary Time consists of seasons between some of the high holy days, the time in which we live most of our lives: between Pentecost and Advent, between Epiphany and Lent. Having the prerogative, I changed the paraments for today.

I find it interesting that the symbol on our banner is a boat. But, it's not a boat sailing on calm, gentle seas. It is the Ark, not the Ark that David carried into Jerusalem and for which Indiana Jones searched. It's Noah's Ark. And though we see the rainbow and the dove there, we can't forget the terrifying experience of the turbulent seas. Life for us is like sailing on the water. There are periods of calm, but you never know when the winds will kick up again, and the waves will swell, and we will be tossed around, fearing for our lives, for our souls.

The symbol for the church has often been a boat on the water – sometimes the Ark, sometimes a small fishing boat, like that of the disciples who were fishermen. Often the mast of that fishing boat looks like a cross. You can see a boat like that on one of the tiles on the steps of the chancel or over the entrance to the sanctuary. Like ours, many churches have been built so that the ceiling looks like an upside-down boat. The part of the building under that ceiling is called the "nave" – which of course has the same root as "naval" or "navy." We are boat people.

The Israelites were not known as seafaring people though. I mean, most of their boats were launched on a relatively small lake, they called the "Sea" of Galilee. They were in-landers for the most part. They had a healthy fear of the sea. Deep water represented chaos to them. In the second verse of Genesis, we're told of the Spirit of God "moving over the face of the waters" before order is established. Several of the Psalms speak of great sea monsters. Sailing the waters was risky business.

In fact, there is hardly a story in the entire Bible about being on the water where it doesn't evoke dread. Think about it. Besides Noah and the flood, there is Jonah, who gets into a storm and is thrown overboard, and swallowed by a great fish. There are the disciples, hauling in the large catch of fish that Jesus has pointed them to, afraid that they will sink under the weight of it. Paul says he was shipwrecked three times. I am not sure why he would keep getting in boats. You get the idea that every time the disciples stepped into a boat, even though some were fishermen, they cast a wary eye toward the heavens. This time was no different.

It was Jesus' suggestion. "Let's go across to the other side," he said- push away from the familiar and head toward something new. It's a leap of faith. Jesus says: "Get in the boat with me." It reminds me of the old story about the guy with the wheelbarrow on the tightrope over Niagara Falls, who walked it across a few times. Then asking who believed he could do it again and getting positive responses, he asked: "Okay, who will get in the wheelbarrow?" [18]

As I said, the Sea of Galilee is hardly a large lake really. But a small boat with a few men rowing could get caught up quickly in a fierce storm coming across the mountains. This was night. No weather reports. Who knew? They'd had such a good day.

Anyone who has ever been in a storm on the water can relate to the fear of the disciples. I once was in a storm on a cruise boat going through the Devil's Triangle. No boat would've been large enough for me then, as it tossed back and forth. In Charleston, I did a funeral for a young man named Breck, whose boat capsized in a squall off the coast. They brought in his body and part of the boat with its name across the bow: "Breck's Joy." We sang the hymn which those who've known the power of the sea first-hand sing so often with quivering voices and tears in their eyes: families of fishermen, of Coast Guard personnel, of sailors, singing that haunting melody, "Eternal Father, strong to save, whose arm has bound the restless wave… O Hear us when we cry to thee for those in peril on the sea." We are boat people.

The great storm comes, the boat is tossed, and Jesus is sleeping. How can he do that? Apparently, the disciples think he can help them if he will. I can't help but think of the prophet Elijah on top of Mt. Carmel taunting the prophets of Baal to call upon their god. "What's the matter?" he asks. "Is your god asleep?" Now, Jesus is asleep. Doesn't he care if we perish? The psalmist in the 10th Psalm asks:

---

[18] cf. Ernest Trice Thompson, *The Face of Faith*, Kohn Printing, Columbia, SC, 1980, pp.3-4.

"Why do you stand far off, O Lord? Why do you hide yourself in times of trouble? Arise, Lord; lift up your hand." The boat is sinking. It's well on its way.

Isn't our God, the One who, as the Psalmist (46) says, "neither slumbers nor sleeps?" Yet sometimes I have felt my life so churned up, so tossed about, so out of my control. Sometimes I've felt I haven't known which way was up. Sometimes, I've felt the dark clouds so heavy over my head, I've wondered if God has forgotten me. There isn't one of us who hasn't known stormy times; not one of us who has only known smooth sailing. The doctor comes in: "It looks suspicious," she says. The company sends a memo: "There's going to be a down-sizing." The principal sends a note: "We're going to have to have a conference." There isn't one of us who hasn't had something at work, something at home, or something in the church; something about our mental, physical or spiritual health or that of people we love.

Some storms last longer than others; some cause more destruction, but we all face them. In that sense we're all in the same boat. The story says Jesus finally awoke and rebuked the wind, and said to the sea, "Peace, be still!" And the wind ceased, and there was a great calm.

The night Hurricane Hugo hit Charleston, I was watching the news. They showed the weather map and this huge storm with its focus on Charleston Harbor. It looked like it was right on top of the home where we'd lived- a feeling in some ways, I've had before. We stayed on the phone to some friends there as long as we could, until the line went down. Through the night, we listened and hoped and prayed as trees fell around them and water rose in the streets.

Then, the eye passed over them and they ran outside to meet and hug others from their neighborhood. Everyone was alright. There was a great calm in the eye of the storm. Then, the winds picked up again. Some storms we get through, frightened but pretty much unscathed.

A woman recently told me she had been so anxious going into surgery, but after we'd prayed together she felt, in her words, "a great calm." I think of some of the storms that have swirled around me, over and over. I've kept hearing Jesus saying: "Why are you afraid? Have you no faith?" The Teacher says, "Remember what I've told you and shown you. Trust me." And I, like the disciples, pray; "Lord increase my faith."

Who is this who calms the winds and the waves? The old hymn says: "Fairest Lord Jesus, ruler of all nature." But the disciples' reaction to Jesus here is really one of awe and fright. It's something like the end of Mark's Gospel where, after all hell has broken loose, Jesus awakes. He finally gets up. They had had high hopes. Those close to Jesus had hopes of something. But confronted with this news, the women at the tomb run away, astonished and trembling. You remember? In the boat, whatever the disciples expected from Jesus, it wasn't this. This is beyond their expectations.

It's a wonderful promise – if you believe it – that Jesus will always be in the boat with us. Some would have you believe that getting in the boat with Jesus will be all smooth- sailing. It's not true. In fact, he is the one the powers and principalities are going to attack most ferociously. On the other side of the lake, demons are waiting.

The apostle Paul said he had suffered shipwreck, exile, beatings and prison in the name of Jesus. At one point he told the Corinthians that he and his group of disciples were "so utterly and unbelievably crushed" that they "despaired of life itself." He said: "We felt that we had received the sentence of death; but that was to make us rely not on ourselves but on God who raises the dead: he delivered us from so deadly a peril, and he will deliver us. On him we have set our hope that he will deliver us again" (1 Corinthians 1:8-10).

What might we be called to face? Who knows. One way or another, we can be certain there will be yet more storms before we're done. It was during the storm he calmed it. He is with us through, not just around the storms. He is with us even through death.

During the storm, we might not receive what we have sought. But we are promised we will receive more than anything we could hope.

Holy Ground
Exodus 3:1-6

I've always been interested in historical markers. It's surprising where they can turn up. You can find them in what you think are some of the most God-forsaken places. I've run across them in fields in the middle of nowhere, and in the heart of big cities, stuck alongside a busy road among tall buildings and flashing signs, covered up by years of forgetfulness. Who would've ever thought something important happened there?

Well, people have been putting up signs of remembrance for generations. When young Jacob left Beer-Sheba and went toward Haran, leaving his family for a new life, he lay down in the desert and put a stone under his head for a pillow. No wonder he had strange dreams. He dreamed of a ladder, a stairway to heaven (remember Led Zeppelin?) with angels going up and down, and a voice from the Lord telling him that God would be with him wherever he went, and one day would bring him back home.

When Jacob awoke, he stood up in that barren place and said, "This is an awesome place! Surely God is here, and I did not know it." He took the stone and set it up as a pillar to mark the place so that those who would pass by after him would take notice…and maybe so that he also might be able to find his way back to this place again and remember he was not alone.

The Israelites, when they finally crossed the Jordan River into the Promised Land, set up stones to mark the spot so that neither they nor others after them would forget what happened there. The prophet Samuel took a rock and set it between Mizpah and Jeshanah, and called the stone Ebenezer, "stone of help," because the Lord had helped the Israelites there in that place in their battle against the

Philistines. So, we sing that strange line in the hymn we sing today: "Here I raise my Ebenezer, hither by Thy help I'm come." An Ebenezer is a stone of remembrance, a physical reminder that God has been with us even in the most desolate places.

Moses walked among the sheep by the side of a mountain where his ancestors had walked and shepherded sheep and worshiped. Who knows what this place meant to him, except a place of refuge from an angry Pharaoh, a place where he was no longer a prince, but in which he had married and had children and a job to do each day, until one day, walking a path he'd probably walked many times, he stopped and looked. There was a bush burning, but not burning up. Because of nothing more than his curiosity perhaps, he didn't just hurry by, but turned aside to study it more closely, to look more deeply. And there, he heard the voice of God telling him: "Take off your shoes, for you're standing on holy ground." Who would've known?

For forty years he would lead a group of ex-slaves who had prayed for and dreamed of coming back to this land of their ancestors. Both Jews and others exiled from it have continued to long for it, longed to walk where their ancestors walked, where God spoke and reached out to them on dusty roads and from burning bushes. Our faith, too, has been tied to this holy land, where God incarnate in Jesus Christ was baptized in the Jordan River, taught by the Sea of Galilee, and was crucified on a hill outside the gates of Jerusalem.

I have an old friend who lives in Washington, D.C. She's a journalist, an author who teaches writing. She came back to Decatur last weekend to speak at the Decatur Book Festival. She read from her book which, in part, tells of the place she grew up- our neighborhood. She'd lived elsewhere for forty years, but it still has a special place in her memory and in her heart; a place that was formative for who she is and what she's done, and what she still longs to do and who she still longs to be. From time to time, I go back there. I ride down the street and stop and look at my old house. I go to the park behind it and walk the ground where I played, where I made my first friendships, where God spoke to me in various ways.

If we are saved anywhere, it happens here, on this good earth, in a place. For Christians, as for many people of other faiths, our faith is tied to places, places where we have felt the extraordinary presence of God during the ordinary- or at least some deep tugging on our heart and soul. It has been felt in places where we have laughed and cried, played and strived, places where we have given birth and buried our loved ones. It is the turf we have prayed over and fought over, our holy land. It's not always the land we would choose, but which has chosen us. It can be a rugged and desolate place, but which for us somehow looks like a land flowing with milk and honey.

Eugene Peterson, professor emeritus of Spiritual Theology at Regent College in Vancouver and the author of more than thirty books on faith and life, tells of a cabin on some lakeshore property in Montana his father bought in 1946. For all the moves he's made over the years, and all the places he's lived, Peterson says he keeps going back to that little cabin. It's a place of hospitality and healing. He says that, "The life of faith cannot be lived in general or by abstractions. All the great realities that we can't touch or see take form on ground that we can touch and see… Place gathers stories, relationships, memories," he says. "And even when I was not there physically, the internalized space grounded me." [19]

Where are your holy places? Where are your touchstones, places where you've raised your Ebenezer, a reminder of where God has come to you to give you comfort or challenge, hope or peace. Where have you been, as the old hymn puts it, "lost in wonder, love and

---

[19] Eugene Peterson, *The Pastor: A Memoir*, Harper One, 2011, pp. 9-14.

praise?" (*Love Divine, All Loves Excelling*). The key, as some would tell us, is in paying attention, in not passing by too hurriedly in our busyness, caught up in the ordinary, dulled by the common place, bored. The poet, Elizabeth Barrett Browning, in those familiar lines said: "Earth's crammed with heaven. And every common bush afire with God; But only he who sees, takes off his shoes; the rest sit around it and pluck blackberries."[20]

In recent years I've become aware that I have lived in Covington longer than I've lived anywhere else in my life. I've watched seedlings grow into huge oak trees in my yard as little children have grown into adults with their own children. I drive streets that have changed more than I can remember and past houses of saints long since gone.

I have been a part of this church longer than I've been a part of any other. I have walked the hallways early in the morning past the eyes of watchful former pastors, and the grounds late at night past the graves of former members. I've eaten countless church dinners in the fellowship hall. I have baptized generations and served communion through numerous seasons. I have done wedding after wedding and funeral after funeral. The walls here are saturated with hymns sung; they are dripping with prayers lifted. Oh, I know you can have church anywhere, but for many through the years, this has been a holy place, a place where God has gotten our attention and called us to all kinds of service in the kingdom.

I suspect heaven looks a lot more like places we've known than pearly gates and golden streets, a place where we'll take off our shoes and walk with the One who makes all our places, all our paths, all things, holy.

---

[20] Elizabeth Barrett Browning, *Aurora Leigh*.

Sighs Too Deep for Words
Psalms 46; Romans 8:18-39

Last week I said, we never know what the day will bring. Who could've imagined? The primary thought I had as the day began Tuesday was not to forget that it was my oldest child's birthday. Now, few of us will ever forget that date. Images have been indelibly printed on our minds: the crashes of the planes, the falling of the towers, the incredible rubble, the billowing smoke and people running, running, covered with soot and ashes, the police and firefighters and medical teams marching back in and searching through the ruins; and heart-sick relatives and friends lined along the streets with pictures of missing loved ones; the Congress of the U.S. on the steps of the capital singing " God Bless America," and the British band in front of Buckingham Palace playing " The Star Spangled Banner," and so many more.

We have been glued to the television. When I went for lunch on Tuesday, not feeling very hungry, but somehow needing to be among people, there was a television at Dot's Country Kitchen and people sat in silence watching. We have walked around dazed, unable to focus on things which once seemed so important. We have broken down in tears. We have screamed in anger. There have been those who've compared this to Pearl Harbor. Most of us were not yet born then. But this time, an enemy unknown to most of us for reasons we can't begin to understand, has attacked the symbols of our prosperity and our might, and thank God, never arrived at the symbol of our government- and thousands, thousands are dead.

We keep watching over and over, the towers standing again on the familiar skyline- as they ought to be- and the planes flying again, and we hope somewhere deep inside this time it won't happen. But, the landscape has been changed- forever changed. We are not the same as we were when we awoke Tuesday morning. We cycle through feelings of fear and grief and anger. Words, words keep coming from those we hope will help us make some sense of it, that will help put the pieces of it back together for us. We are experiencing some of what much of the world has already known. And certainly, we will need to be more attuned to circumstances in the world which generate such insane rage.

I drove to Conyers Tuesday night just after 6:00 p.m., down streets eerily empty for that time of evening, and gathered with other Presbyterians- as one needing to hear more than I needed to speak. I have helped lead three worship services before this one, and I tell you, I have looked forward more to praying than to preaching; for at least I've held on to those comforting words of Paul's to the church in Rome: " The Spirit helps us in our weakness, for we do not know how to pray as we ought, but that very Spirit intercedes for us with sighs too deep for words" (Romans 8: 26).

I turned down the sound on the television and just watched the pictures and sighed. It is too deep for words. What we need most of all, is to come together and to be reassured of the presence of God among us. Yet, too, we need to keep talking- telling stories which will help us through it. Telling so we don't forget- so we'll never forget.

It has touched us all- not just those in New York and Washington and Philadelphia. It's not like a moment when one or a few of us feel the weight of tragedy. We are in this together and that is both the horror and the grace of it. I don't mean to say that we have been victims in the same sense as those lost in the plane crash in Pennsylvania, or had offices in those buildings, or just happened to be in the wrong place at the wrong time. But, we are victims in that we are not free as we once were. We will know it every time we want to fly on an airplane, every time we want to gather at a large public event, every time we want to visit a national landmark. If the Pentagon isn't safe, what is?

Already there are Americans, some Muslims, some with roots in the Middle East who are looked upon with suspicion and ill will. All of this can either bring out the best or the worst in us. It has touched us all. As the hours and days go on, as crews search in the ruins, more and more stories will be uncovered, some horrible, but some wonderful, some strange, but some amazing, some accounts of cowardice and hatred but also many of heroism and compassion.

There are stories of our own. I have cousins in New York City. Others of you have relatives there. A close friend of my brother-in-law e-mailed him from a hospital in New York City. He was there with his young daughter who had gone for a desperate operation- scheduled that morning. They watched from their windows as the Trade Center crumbled. Her surgery has been postponed indefinitely. Sam Hay III was in the World Trade Center six days before. He stood with a man whose office on the 88th floor was covered with pictures of his family. As they stood together looking out across the magnificent view, the man said his children had called him from the Statue of Liberty the week before and said they were waving at him. Finally, on Friday Sam got word, his friend had made it out.

But John Towler lost his entire office he once worked with. All 16 are unaccounted for- and 300 of the 600 in the company are missing and the man who took John's place is gone. Melissa Roberts, daughter of Robby and Laura, was on her way to an interview in the tower that morning. The buildings were on fire as she emerged from the subway. A woman she didn't know (an angel she wonders?) grabbed her hand and they ran to safety, covered with ashes, praying out loud. A family member of Rita Harrel's son was also on the streets below running for safety. Cindy Moon is a flight attendant-with all the anxiety of that currently. A member in her extended family was the architect for the World Trade Center.

Others in our congregation were diverted from their destinations: the McGibonys and the Howards were delayed in Ireland. The Stamps were diverted to a military base in Nova Scotia. Their son who works in the Pentagon was not there that day. Hughie Hudson's son, Lelia's brother, was there working in the Pentagon. Roger Tingler had been in Washington at the Senate Building and Chris Gwinn at the State Department Building. Mark Burton, Allene's son, has gone to work with a medical team there. Others, children of the church, are in the armed services on alert. There are others of you with stories.

Many of us have been to New York and Washington. We have memories of being there. I can remember sitting in the observation deck of the World Trade Center and tentatively looking down- looking down on lines of tiny cars, and specks of people scurrying along- our busiest city. I remember looking down, too, on the Cathedral of St. John the Divine, the beautiful cathedral which takes in many of the poor from the streets. I wonder what's happened to it.

Buildings crumble, lives can be taken. But, I am reminded of an older pastor, a friend, who after Hurricane Hugo had damaged much of Charleston, made his way to his church. Walking through water and debris, he came up to the pulpit, the Bible still open on it. He turned to the scripture and with several of the congregation out in the water, he read from Isaiah: "The grass withers, the flower fades but the Word of God shall stand forever." When all our words fail us, the Word of God comes to those who have ears to hear, enabling us to cry out as others before us in times of crisis gone by. The psalmist says: "God is our refuge and strength, a very present help in trouble. Therefore, we will not fear though the earth should change, though the mountains shake in the heart of the sea…Be still and know that I am God…The Lord of hosts is with us, the God of Jacob is our refuge."

The Apostle Paul, who knew a lot about suffering and hatred, speaking to the Christians in Rome said, "The whole world groans in travail" but "in everything, God works for good" to give birth to hope. Not that there isn't suffering now, isn't hurt now, but that we live according to a sure promise, that suffering, and evil do not have the last word; that the supreme symbol for us is the cross, and the last word is resurrection, life which rises from the ashes of death.

"What then shall we say to this?" Paul asks. "I am sure that neither death nor life, nor angels, nor rulers, nor things present, nor things to come, nor powers, nor height, nor depth, nor anything else in all creation, will be able to separate us from the love of God in Christ Jesus our Lord." In that knowledge we can live each day, not bowing to evil, not giving it its due. Nor do we let ourselves succumb to all the solutions the world offers; not trying to overcome evil with evil, but with good (Romans 12:2).

We follow the One who loves the world and who seeks its redemption; who offers justice and gives peace beyond our understanding. We follow the One who calls us to obedience and sacrifice, who makes the claim that to trust in anything else but him is empty and futile. Hear his invitation: To all who have been unable to pray, to all who sigh for lack of words, come to a place where the Spirit intercedes for us; come to hear a Word of hope from beyond ourselves; come to be a part of a community built on a firm foundation; come to receive new life through the One whose holy body has been broken for us, whose blood has been poured out for us and for all this groaning world.

Why Church?

John 15:4-5; Ephesians 1:15-23

We were eating on an outside patio of a restaurant, on Church Street, looking right across at the church where I grew up. It's changed a lot since then, as the city has changed, as it's grown up around the church. There are restaurants and high-rise condos, and the MARTA station.

As we watched there were people sitting on the benches in the church yard and passing by on the sidewalks – a busy night life. It reminded me that churches were put up at crossroads in the midst of banks and businesses, courthouses and government buildings to make the statement that God is active in the world, and for the World, and calls us to be also. The Gospel is good news for this life, not a retreat from it.

I remembered the church – this church – as a place I was baptized; where my parents brought me, knowing that they couldn't raise me and my sisters by themselves; knowing they needed help with such a frightening and wonderful responsibility, help not only from God but from others who would make holy promises to teach us about God's love, to remind us that no matter how far we wandered, we'd always be God's children. They took us there regularly, knowing that we couldn't get there on our own, and that it was too important for us to miss.

What they did wasn't only for us, but for themselves as well, because of the hunger in their own hearts, the thirst in their own souls. So, we learned in Sunday school the stories of Jesus and of God's people, and that we were part of that long line of witnesses. We sang the hymns, lyrics and melodies that still come back to me in my times of greatest distress and times of greatest joy.

The church is people, first, and not a building, but it is, for us, a holy place – or holy places, since some of us have been a part of several of them. The church is a place where we meet some people we normally wouldn't have met and might have had no desire to meet. We meet them because God called us there. The church isn't a voluntary association. It's a place where the walls and ceilings are saturated with the prayers of those who only by God's grace, and only together are saints. It's a place where we learn a different language – a language foreign to much of the world – the language of confession and forgiveness, redemption and resurrection; where we are fed the bread of life and offered the cup of salvation and from where we are sent out into the world every week with God's power and blessing. You see, it was not primarily some lone voice in my head, or coming from the sky, calling me into ministry. It came through the church, and was confirmed by the church, through the voice of others of God's children.

As I thought about my church, growing up, I thought of people who passed in and out of those doors. Of course, we all come and go eventually, one way or another. But for some, the things that rooted me never seemed to take root in them. For some, the ties did not bind, and they drifted away for one reason or another.

As a pastor, I have a passion to help bind people to the church – not as some duty or obligation; not as a matter of guilt; not as something we do to win God's favor. But because, as the Psalmist says, our souls "thirst for the Living God" (Psalms 42:2); because we enter the house of the Lord "with glad shouts and songs of thanksgiving, a multitude keeping festival (Psalms 42:4); because, as Jesus said, "I am the vine, you are the branches… separated from me you can do nothing" (John 15:5).

It's a communal image. You see, to be attached to Jesus, is to be attached to others. To separate ourselves from God's people is to separate ourselves from him. Our discipleship isn't based on our race, our gender, or our heritage, not on our commonality of interests or hobbies or our shared views of politics or ideology, but rather on our common connection to Jesus Christ.

That doesn't mean it's always easy. This vine imagery can call to mind all kinds of entanglements. But as one of you told this congregation a couple of years ago during stewardship season, "I'm not Christian without you."

Jesus didn't just do individual spiritual mentoring; he called disciples into a new community, which is a great blessing. It's different from every other organization, but it is an organization. People of course are always coming in and out of a church. Work, life, take people to other places. Sickness, disability keep some from joining in certain parts of the church's life and fellowship. We've lost so many wonderful, gifted people through the years. God continually sends us out to do new work.

But, too, some people leave because they're angry – angry at God or at the denomination. Or they leave because they're angry at somebody in the congregation. They leave with hurt feelings. It's not easy trying to live out our faith together. Some people leave because they look around and no longer see their best friends, or because they never really bonded with those here with them. For some, it's a change of priorities in their lives. Some just seem to get out of the habit and drift away. Some never say why they have left and I'm not always sure they could articulate it.

Statistics show that most people who leave Presbyterian churches don't end up going to any church. And that, I believe is the saddest part of all. Calvin and Luther said, there was no "ordinary" salvation outside the church. Which means, it's extraordinary if we can really live a life of faith outside the church. Of course, God's Church, "the holy catholic" or "universal church" as we say in the creed, is much larger than any individual church or denomination – or even religion. Jesus said, "I have other sheep who are not of this fold" (John 10:16). Jesus is active outside this church – any church.

People say sometimes, "I'm spiritual, I'm just not religious." Now, our personal spirituality is important, but some people sometimes seem to take a little of this and a little of that and make it whatever they want it to be.

It's within a fellowship of believers that we study the Word and act as checks and balances to our individual interpretations. Otherwise God's voice can begin to sound a whole lot like our own.

The thing is, without others of the body of Christ, we tend to make up our own religion. Oh, we still do that when part of a fellowship of believers; it's just harder. I can worship God on a mountain trail or on the beach by myself – and I do, but not for long. Jesus said, "Where 2 or 3 are gathered, there I am in the midst of you." When Paul and the first disciples went out to proclaim the Gospel, they started churches. Paul called them Christ's body in the world.

Now, some folks will say, "I have my church: my friends, my family." Well, maybe, but the church is where the Word is regularly read and studied, where the sacraments are shared, and holy promises are made, where prayers are regularly lifted with and for one another. It's where we worship with others. It's God's people, God's Church. Corporate worship is at the very heart of our faith – always has been. As the Presbyterian *Book of Common Worship* says, "Worship is the principal influence that shapes our faith and the most visible way we express our faith." It's the most distinctive act of faith. It's where we're reminded that our chief end, our highest priority, is "to glorify God and enjoy God forever" (*The Shorter*

Catechism, answer 1). Which means not so much what we do, but what we open ourselves to God doing in us and for us.

We're entering the season of Lent. Traditionally, for Christians, Lent has been a time for preparation and discernment, a time for discipline (not often one of our favorite words), a time for spiritual practices that will move us closer to God and God's people. It's a time for seeking God's help in giving up some things: bad habits, lazy discipleship, attitudes that are less than loving. It's a time for giving up the idea that we can live life on our own, in our own way. It's also a season to practice the discipline of taking on things: prayer, meditation, service, the reading of God's Word and worship – things we've neglected.

It's a time for seeking to give ourselves more to the One who has given himself first to us. He is the vine through whom we are connected to God and to one another, so that we may bear fruit, becoming more and more, the ones God intends us to be.

Go Figure

1 Timothy 6:6-8, 17-19; 2 Corinthians 8:1-15

"Sharing" is at the top of the list of those things Robert Fulghum claims we learned—or should've learned—in the sand pile at kindergarten.[21] The Apostle Paul tells about it here in his first letter to Timothy, the young disciple who sits in the theological sand pile. Paul tells him what it takes to be content, how much is enough in the economy of the One "who richly furnishes us with everything to enjoy." He says that to be liberal (generous) is to discover what life is about.

When it comes to sharing, I don't know of any other passage in Scripture that is more remarkable than this one. I've returned to it again and again because it's so rich in wisdom on the subject. Paul says to the Corinthians (just after this): "O, I know you don't really need to hear this. I know you're ready and eager" —but he goes on to tell them anyway, just for good measure. That's the way I feel in preaching stewardship sermons: You know all this—you live it, no doubt better than I do, but for all our sakes, I'll say it again.

Listen: 1 Timothy 6:6-8, 17-19; 2 Corinthians 8:1-15.

It's all over the news. It's everywhere you turn: anxiety about the economy, Freddie Mac, Fannie Mae, banks going under, houses in foreclosure, long gas lines, rising fuel prices, stock market tumbles, jobs being lost, federal bailouts. We have lots of anxiety about these things. Meanwhile, the Food Pantry is being flooded, and Faith Works which helps people with basic rent and utilities in Jesus'

---

[21] Robert Fulghum, *All I Really Need to Know I Learned in Kindergarten: Uncommon Thoughts on Common Things*, Villard Books, New York, 1989.

name, and ours, keeps closing its doors for lack of enough funds to meet the overwhelming demands.

So, it might well seem that we're in a rather precarious position in starting to talk about raising money in the church. Maybe we just ought to forget it this year and hope for better days to come down the road. Or maybe the government really will bail us out. I don't have any answer as far as the economy goes. I don't think anybody really does. And I'm going to tell you right up front, I'm not much of a fundraiser. I'm not all that good with figures. I'm not an accountant, I'm a preacher.

But, the Bible's not all that good with figures either, it seems. I mean, Jesus told people to forgive one another 70 x 7. Do you think he really meant 490 times-exactly? Do you think it rained on Noah 40 days, and Moses was on the mountain 40 days and Jesus was in the wilderness 40 days, and the Hebrew children wandered in the desert 40 years, and David reigned over Israel 40 years? Or do the scriptures just mean it was a long time, a holy time? Did Jesus feed 5,000 people, or as Matthew says, was it 5,000 men and some women and children, and did Jesus send out his disciples to count them all? Or is the point that there were a whole lot of folks, fed by what didn't seem enough, and even plenty to spare? How does that work: 2 fishes, 1 loaf-5,000 or so fed? And what about Jesus' story of the sower who spreads a little seed here and a little seed there, much of it falling on barren ground—and yet it grows up 30-60-100-fold? It doesn't add up.

By my reading, most often when numbers are mentioned in the Bible, 3-7-40-5,000 or whatever, it's usually a matter of faith, not math. If you start trying to add it all up, in the usual way, it just won't make sense. But, if we're thinking about what we must work with and what God wants us to do with it…well, there's no limit—no limit at all.

Now, let's be clear. I'm not just talking about seeds or loaves and fishes. I'm talking about money—real money. It's been pointed out—again, I'm not that good with figures—but somebody apparently has counted and says that 1 of every 6 verses in the Bible has to do with money. Jesus talked about it a lot. Thirteen of his 18 parables have to do with money. It was his second favorite topic, next to the Kingdom of God. So, I don't get it when people say: "I wish they wouldn't be talking about money in church so often." Hey, we're trying to follow Jesus. And at times, it almost seems like he said: "If you want to be my disciple, pick up your cash and follow me."

You know, the church often wrangles over things Jesus never mentioned and ignores most of what he talked about so often. There is nothing in the Bible people agree on more not to take literally than what Jesus said about money. What we do with money probably says more about what we truly believe than anything else we do.

Now, you know all this—I don't need to tell you, but, indulge me. Let me remind us all. The Gospel is good news. Sometimes—sometimes- we lose sight of that. We get wrapped up in things and anxious, and we need to hear again what Paul says life is about. We need to be reminded of what God can do in us and through us.

I need to be reminded, especially in times like these. So, I've gone back to the words of that old preacher, Paul. There is a lot in here we can take to the bank, so to speak. He begins his stewardship message to the folks in Corinth by talking about the grace of God and how that's been shown in their brothers and sisters over in Macedonia. In their severe conditions, "their extreme poverty has overflowed in a wealth of liberality. They begged us," he says, "for the favor of giving." Isn't that incredible? It doesn't add up. But, Gallup Polls continually have told us that poorer people in this country give away a greater percent of their income to charity than do others with more money. Go figure. Remember Jesus and the widow who put her coin in the offering? He said she gave more than all the others.

Recently, I went over to Covington Manor to visit some of our folks in the nursing home. I tend to get most of my news from Sarah Hooten. This day, I found her in her room, in front of the T.V., which was loud enough to blast the windows out. She was watching one of those game shows where people jump around like idiots at the prospect of winning money. Somebody was trying to win a million dollars. I asked her what she'd do if she won a million dollars. She looked at me and said: "I'd find somebody who really needed it and give it away." Again, as Paul says: You can't take it with you. And what life's really all about has a lot to do with sharing.

Now, after telling the Corinthians about the incredible generosity of the Macedonians, he goes on to assure them that he's not asking them to burden themselves too greatly to ease the situation of some others, but that as a matter of "equality," their abundance now, should supply the great need of others. Jesus hasn't called us to be comfortable in our discipleship. There's always risk, always some growing pains. Following Jesus comes at some real cost. So, we're not just asked to give out of our surplus, or even as sporadic acts of charity, but as a disciplined, ongoing stewardship. If it doesn't cost us something, in the way we live our lives, if there are not some things we can't do because we've elected to share what we've been given, then we're probably not being that faithful.

But, this is what Paul goes on to say. He says that the ones with more now give to others to supply their needs so that their abundance (that's the "abundance" of the poor folks) will supply the need of the richer folks. Now isn't that something? Paul suggests there is something that poorer folks might have to share with richer folks. Which kind of puts another spin on the expression, "There but for the grace of God go I." Maybe it has to do with knowing how to live on less—joyfully, abundantly, gratefully. Not that all poor folks know that, but that there are those who know what it is to be content and to live in the richness of God.

Shane Claiborne, who has lived among some of the poorest people in the world, working with Mother Teresa, tells of giving an ice cream cone to one of the children on the streets of Calcutta. It was his birthday. It was 120 degrees. When the child looked at the ice cream, he literally shook with excitement. He took the cone, but before taking his first lick, he yelled to other children around him: "We have ice cream!" They all lined up for a lick.[22]

All that we have, we hold in trust, from the One who is the giver of all good gifts. We have this stewardship. What we do with the money we have is a matter of faith. How much do we value the cause of the Church of Christ? We're not encouraged to give just because we have bills to pay. It's not just about raising funds, so I and the Session don't have to be fundraisers. As Paul says about the "poor" Macedonians, "First of all, they gave themselves to the Lord and then to the Lord's people." In this church, we don't set a budget and then say, "This is just exactly what we need." We hold up the opportunity to those whose hearts belong to God and who beg for the favor of giving, and then we encourage one another to imagine what God can do through us. It's not necessarily good math, but it is good faith. But then, I don't really have to tell you this, do I?

---

[22] Shane Claiborne in an address to the Church Unbound Conference in Montreat, NC, 2008.

Patriotism

Matthew 5:14-16; Philippians 3:17-21

The reading from Matthew is part of Jesus' most remembered words, what we know as the Sermon on the Mount. These words come after Jesus has called his disciples "the salt of the earth." Here, he calls them "the light of the world." It is his light they are to let shine through them for the salvation of the world.

In his Letter to the Philippians, Paul speaks of their "pressing on toward the goal for the prize of the upward call of God in Christ." He says," imitate me." He offers himself as an example of how to live as a follower of Christ. He reminds them that they are citizens of heaven.

We had a stop-over in Salt Lake City a couple of months ago on our way to Jackson Hole and our beautiful National Park, Yellowstone. As we curled in for our approach to the airport, we flew low over the Great Salt Lake and the Bonneville Salt Flats. My father was stationed at Wendover Field there for a short time before being deployed to England during World War II.

There is a picture in the bookcase in our den of him and my mother just after they were married there, sitting on top of a little rugged mountain, looking over those salt flats, Dad in his Army Air Corp uniform and Mom wrapped in the coat he was issued. They had grown up together in Clinton, SC, on the campus of Presbyterian College. They had known each other since they were children, but she had taken a train all by herself, all the way out there to this desolate area of Utah for her wedding, with nobody else she knew there except my Dad.

My mother and my aunt lived with my grandparents while they waited for their husbands to return from opposite sides of the world, engaged in wars with two different enemies. Daddy returned three years later to a toddler, my oldest sister. Was it harder for those who went or for those who waited on them, those who served in their own ways? I don't know. Some of you have a better idea of that.

My father had dodged bombs. He said that when the whistling stopped, you had better be under cover. His group had 524 killed in action, 801 taken prisoner, 2 missing. It was a world I can only imagine through pictures and the stories they told. But, I know because of what they did, during what they had to live through, my world has been different then what it could've been. And I am grateful.

Largely through my father, I have a certain view of patriotism. I don't remember him dressing up in red, white and blue or waving flags much. I do remember working with him on every Fourth of July to secure the flag on the side of the house. If it began to rain, we had to take it down quickly. When the flag was presented in public and the National Anthem sung, he stood with his hand over his heart. I never remember him saying anything to or about others who didn't do that. It was his example that influenced me.

It's been said that a symbol is a physical sign of a deeper reality, which speaks to the heart maybe more than to the mind. The American flag is probably the supreme symbol of this nation, and it evokes deep emotions. I have to say I'm a little uneasy when I see people wrapping themselves in the flag: literally dressing themselves in flag bathing suits, for instance. I saw a guy on the beach this Fourth of July wearing a flag speedo- a *tiny* speedo. I won't tell you the things that came to my mind. When I think of being wrapped in the flag, first I think of those shipped home in flag-draped caskets.

Neither am I fond of using the flag for simple advertising. I get almost as uneasy with somebody surrounded by flags giving me a sales pitch as I do somebody passing himself off as a "Christian plumber" or whatever. At times I feel like some people shake the flag in others' faces like there's some way you're supposed to show your patriotism. I feel it's too often used as a political statement, to stress a political view. But, as Navy Chaplain, Margaret Grun Josselyn has said: "In recognition of individual consciences and judgement, patriotism cannot be made the exclusive property of any class, group or school of thought."[23] Nobody has a lock on patriotism.

If it's love of country that inspires patriotism, why do we love our country? Because it's beautiful? Because of its amber waves of grain, its purple mountain majesties, its shining seas? Certainly, it's beautiful. But, other countries are beautiful, too: The Alps, the Himalayas, the Andes, the Mediterranean beaches, the rain forests are found in other countries.

Is it the government we love? Well, yes and no. Most of us would say it's the best way to do it. But, we're constantly critical of our government, often depending on who's running it now.

Is it the people? Do we really have better people than other countries do? People of other countries love one another. There are people I love who are citizens of other countries, smart people, loving people, faithful people; a great many of them are not shooting one another at nearly the rate we are.

Is it because we're free? Free to do what- whatever we want? There are plenty of other people in the world who are free.

---

[23] Margaret Grun Josselyn, "Patriotism: Will it Preach?" *Journal for Preachers*, Pentecost 1990, pp. 11-18.

I would say we love this country because it's our country, the place we've grown up, the land on which we've lived, the people we've loved most. The closer we draw our circles, the more intense our love. But, is our patriotism a matter of ideals and principles for which we stand? The truth is, we disagree vehemently, sometimes violently, on many of those things, or how we interpret them.

Some have said we live in a time when the center which once held us together is being strained. I would say we live by words with implications often beyond the understanding of those who first penned ideas like: "all men are created equal." Like with those who wrote the Bible, their words keep pointing beyond the understanding of those of us still trying to live by them. Which is why I still stand with my hand on my heart for the presentation of the flag and the singing of the National Anthem, though I do believe there are injustices, long and deep, which we have failed and still fail to rectify. I confess I'm half-blind at best in recognizing them, and often less than courageous or faithful in confronting them.

Jim Wright, a retired Navy veteran, came home recently from a family picnic on the Blackwater River to find his inbox overflowing with comments and questions. Several people wanted to know what he thought, particularly as a veteran. In short, he posted on his Facebook page that respect can't be compelled, bought or inherited. It can't be demanded by the nozzle of a gun, by beating, shaming or harassing anybody into it. That might be how some countries do it, but it's not what this country is about. He said, it's not love it, like some think you ought to love it, or else you need to leave it. That's not, he says, "why I swore an oath to my country and put my life on the line."

He says, "To you the National Anthem means one thing, to another it means something else. We are all shaped and defined by our experiences and we see the world through our own eyes. That's freedom; that's liberty. The right to believe differently; the right to protest as you will. The right to demand better. The right to believe your country can be better, that it can live up to its sacred ideals, and the right to loudly note it has not. The right to use your voice, your actions, to bring attention to the things you believe in. The right to want more for others, freedom, liberty, justice, equality, and RESPECT." He says, "A true veteran might not agree with the way some go about it, but a true veteran would fight to the death to protect their right to say what they believe."[24]

He calls us to prove others wrong by being people we're called to be. I stand up because I believe in the principles that run deeper than how we often live in this country. That was basic to the Civil Rights movement, the call to live into our best American principles, and to live into our faith.

In 1630, aboard the *Arbela*, the future governor of the Massachusetts Bay Colony, John Winthrop, referred to Jesus' Sermon on the Mount, applying it to the new land to which they approached: "We shall be as a city upon a hill; the eyes of all people are upon us." We certainly have not always lived up to that, as the Native Americans and others later brought here in chains could testify. But, several presidents since have turned to that same biblical passage to provide a vision for the people.

The Apostle Paul claimed his Roman citizenship and preached about being good citizens. He, like his Lord, also died at the hands of the state. Paul said, our commonwealth is in heaven. Our first citizenship is beyond this world. That is what guides us in our living here and now, if we seek to be followers of Jesus. That is what I've taken most

---

[24] Jim Wright, Facebook post, 8/29/16 printed in his blog, "Stone Kettle Station and American News X."

importantly from my father as well. He knew where his priorities lay. He knew to whom he first belonged.

Margaret Grun Josselyn, the Navy Chaplain, again says that patriotism is best expressed in devotion and service, not just limited to military service. Our faith, I believe, might call us to speak for something, to stand for something, to sit for something, to march for something in God's name. The Chaplain says, "Our responsibility is not simply for ourselves, but for our ideals and for all people. If we are bound by national or state lines, we neglect God's purpose…the 'heroes' are those who not only 'love country more than self' but who sacrifice their lives for God that God's mercy may be known by all people." [25]

So, let our light shine, that all may see our good works, as the Apostle Paul says, and give the glory to God.

---

[25] Margaret Grun Josselyn, op. cit., p.13.

What Holds Us Together
Romans 12: 9-21

I've found that a number of couples choose this passage to be read at their wedding. It speaks to living in proximity with somebody who will have different ideas, different ways of doing things, and how we live with that person and still love that person. The Apostle Paul is writing here to the church-that part of the body of Christ in Rome, a city at the center of the world. He is instructing them on how to live out their faith, first as part of the church and then as part of a wider, diverse community. He tells them what genuine love looks like.

Listen: Romans 12: 9-21.

These are contentious times: from North Korea to Russia, to Iran, to Syria, to Washington D.C., to the Georgia capital and Newton County. The other night as Theodosia and I were walking around the square, a pick-up truck with political statements tattooed on it, and an American flag hanging out the back, gunned its engine as some young men yelled at people they passed. We've had guns on the square and a packed house of very angry citizens at County Commission meetings. During recent presidential elections, political signs in my neighborhood were torn up or stolen. On Facebook virtual enemies have been made from real friends.

I saw a cartoon that looked like a Jeopardy Game Show. The host was explaining to one of the contestants: "I know you buzzed in first, but she shouted over you the loudest". [26] We know that if you want to keep your friends and not tear up your family, you don't talk about politics or religion- even in church. That is, we better be careful; how we talk about what faith might lead us to do can also splinter us- and has. I don't mean just this church, but the larger Church, the parts of the one body of Christ.

---

[26] *The New Yorker.*

World-known theologian and former Columbia Theological Seminary professor, Walter Brueggemann, says that the difficulty of speaking out as Christians is that the center no longer holds. Where once we could count on some political and theological assumptions to be widely shared (certainly in this country), that is no longer the case. The division of right and left is so acute; the only common view is a failed public.[27] I've heard suggested that if we could calmly sit down together and look at the facts, rather than just hurling sound bites at one another, we might be able to make some progress. But now we argue over what the facts are, what is true. As noted by President Trump recently: "Nobody knew health care could be so complicated."

I read about a minister who instituted a practice in his church like that used in 12-step or recovery groups. Each person in the group was given a time to speak within an agreed upon time limit. Others had to listen. The usual folks couldn't control the air waves. They couldn't comment or applaud. They could only say "thanks". Some of the folks experiencing it said it was like they were letting God be part of it, like letting God be God.[28]

Douglas, in his book, says we shouldn't be afraid to believe out loud. We're called by God to it. But, he says, it's not just about collecting and presenting facts, but about testifying to our faith; engaging in true conversation in which we "ask more questions, look for more sides, make wider connections.... recognize the limits of our vision.... (and are) surprised by the new things that we (might) see".[29] What Paul says here to the church in Rome is that there are

---

[27] Mark Douglas, *Believing Aloud: Reflections on Being Religious in the Public Square*, Cascade Books, Eugene, Oregon, 2010, p, vii.

[28] Anthony Robinson, "The 'No Cross' Rule", *The Christian Century*, May 10, 2017, pp 10-11.

[29] Mark Douglas. op. cit., p. 139.

certain basics for us as Christians that should hold us together and maybe, by God's grace, hold together much of the wider community.

We are called, as Paul says earlier in this chapter, not to be conformed to this world, but transformed by our faith. We live in this world, this country, but our ultimate allegiance is to a higher authority. We have a different vision from that of much of the world. We are to hate evil –not people-and to hold onto what is good. We are to be aglow in the Spirit. But we are called not to be too haughty, to think too highly of ourselves -like we have all the answers   We are to radiate genuine love- not just what passes for love oftentimes; not just what is experienced in feelings, but which is shown in actions. We are to contribute to the needs of others, to practice hospitality to strangers, to treat one another with affection, to show honor, respect. We are to repay no one evil for evil. So far as it depends on us, we are to live peaceably with all. This is the politics of the kingdom. Paul says, it will require of us to be patient in tribulation (suffering) and constant in prayer.

Joshua Dubois had been praying all night. He was the Executive Director of the White House Office of Faith Based and Neighborhood Partnerships during President Obama's first term. In a book of devotionals, based on the ones he sent every morning to the president, he asks what you do when you disagree with your boss, especially if it's the President of the U.S. The issue concerned the Affordable Care Act, part of which was to make preventative services, including contraception, free for millions of American women, paid for by their employers. He had no problem with that. The problem for Dubois had to do with whether employers who objected to contraception on religious grounds (like the Catholic Church) would have to pay for it. For him, it was a matter of religious liberty, an historic breach of relationship with the church—a matter much bigger than just that particular issue.

There was a great divide on this not only in the country, but in the White House. When it looked like the President would give his support to it, Dubois was angry. He believed others had manipulated the President, that they didn't understand how important this was; that they never wanted what was right; they only wanted to win. He sat down with a senior staffer and railed about it. The veteran staffer listened calmly, then said he understood why he was upset. But, he said, as passionately and angry and hurt as Dubois felt, there were people on the other side who felt just as passionately and would have been just as angry and hurt if it had gone the other way. He said: "Joshua, faith is a big part of your context…but other people have other contexts". He said, for some people he'd known for over 20 years, to reject this would be unthinkable (even unfaithful). He said, you can question political decisions; you can disagree with people vehemently; but you should be very careful before you question others' motives. There are others who do care deeply about the President, about the country, about all those affected. They just end up in a different place. Would it be fair if others questioned your motives?

Dubois said he was still angry, still confident in his position, but he started to realize that one of the great things about this country is that it allows for this kind of disagreement. He said, from then on, he knew his job was "to fight as hard as he could, as fairly as he could; and in the meantime, to love every person he met. And let God work out the rest". [30] "Rejoice in your hope," Paul says. God is the One who will have the last word.

Now, let me say, I'm as prone to flair ups of anger and sarcasm as the next person- even with people I love dearly. My view is that my politics comes out of my faith- and I think at times: if only Christians knew the Bible. I can't for the life of me see how Christian faith can lead others to different conclusions than mine. After all, I'm paid to discern the will of God. I don't see how anybody with any sense could see things differently. But, I know, too, that God is a God of surprises and none of us has the whole truth. We are told not to think of ourselves as wiser than we are.

---

[30] Joshua Dubois, "On Disagreement," *The President's Devotional*, Harper Row, July 2013.

I was thinking about all this not long ago as I was working in the yard. My next-door neighbor has been there for almost 30 years now. He didn't build there because we were next door. He's my neighbor just because he ended up there, and I suppose at times he wishes he hadn't. He's on the other side of the fence from me when it comes to a lot of things. Not a material fence; we've gone back and forth, from yard to yard, house to house, over the years. I have to step past one of his cars that has a bumper sticker that offends me. I've thought I might replace it with another sometime when he is gone.

When he's on vacation, I deliver his mail to his garage. I have his garage door code, which also comes in handy when I want to borrow some tools. When he put his house up for sale, we hung out our laundry in the side yard. He gave up trying to move. When our beloved dog died, he dug the grave and stepped up to pray when I couldn't. If I'm in trouble, I know he'll be the first to come help me: one, because he is right next door, and being retired, he's usually there; two, because he'd do it for any human being. Then, there's that we're both Clemson fans. But most of all because despite some of our differences, by the grace of God, we've now become old friends. Thanks be to God.

Foolishness
1 Corinthians 1:18-31

"What do you do during the week, Mr. Billy?" That's the question she asked me, a child of the church. It wasn't the first time I've been asked that, of course. I've been asked that plenty of times by adults. It's a pretty common joke: "What do you preachers do the rest of the week, when you're not preaching?" My children – grown children- will still call sometimes and say, "Dad, what are you doing?" And I'll say, "Nothing, just waiting for you to call."

This little girl was serious. So, I tried to tell her. Oh, I do weddings, you know; I meet with couples to talk about marriage and plan their service. I do funerals and I meet with those folks. I get the bulletins ready for Sunday, maybe prepare a Sunday school lesson or teach a Bible study. And of course, there's the sermon. That takes time. I don't just walk up and start preaching on Sunday. I visit folks: sick folks, new folks, older folks. And I go to meetings- you wouldn't believe how many meetings. And …. well…. there are lots of other things I do that are hard to explain, I tried to explain. But her interest had trailed off long before that.

I wonder sometimes myself what I do. Years ago, I came in one morning. I parked in the gravel lot that was there before we built the playground and all that. There were a bunch of monks with their brown robes hiked up, smoking cigarettes on the back steps. After a minute, I figured they must be characters from the *In the Heat of the Night* television show. But, I'm sometimes the last to know some things around here. I wondered what people passing by were thinking.

But, you never know who's coming to the door of the church. Not long ago, I came in a little early. Immediately, the doorbell started buzzing and kept buzzing from one of the regulars. The telephone started ringing, and there was a guy sleeping at the side door. There also were some others trying to get in to fix the air conditioning. Usually I pass a lot of things off to Peni and Dan, because they know a lot more things than I do and can really help some people. After all that, I started going through my e-mails and listening to messages on the telephone. It was a pretty ordinary day- just beginning. I guess it doesn't sound like winning the world.

Michael Thompson asked me not long-ago what things might be needed to add to the list of duties for the new interim pastor. Hmmmm... The Apostle Paul said, "Not many of you were wise, but God chose what is foolish in the world..." That's sort of comforting. I'm reminded of the minister who had just gotten a new doctoral degree. Somebody from the church called his home asking for Dr. Jones (emphasizing the title). His young daughter answered and said: "Well, I guess you meant my daddy, but I can tell you right now, Mr., he's not the kind of doctor that'll do you any good." (Michael Jenkins?) Once when my children were young teens, somebody called the house. My middle child answered and came down the steps to tell me. He said: "Dad, it's an old lady who says she needs to talk with you. But I don't know what you can do for her. Sounds like she needs a doctor."

It's hard to explain sometimes; and these verses from Paul's letter to the Corinthians seem strangely appropriate: "Consider your call.... God chose what is foolish in the world..." You see, Paul was trying to explain his own ministry. He was trying to tell the people in Corinth what it means to be a minister of the Gospel. He was trying to say something about the Gospel itself. And what he said was that the Gospel often sounds like foolishness, and those who believe it often look like fools. Now, that's not to say we aren't really fools sometimes, and that some things we spend our time and energy on are not truly foolishness. But, it is to say that there are things which by the world's standards often seem unimportant and people who often seem unimportant, but which are precisely those things by which the kingdom comes.

The world did not know God through wisdom, Paul says, "but it pleased God through the folly of what we preach to save those who believe." Through us it's proclaimed, in all our stumbling, bumbling ways. And exactly what do we proclaim? That the last shall be first and the first last; that it's better to give than to receive; that the meek shall inherit the earth; that we are to pray for our persecutors, and love our enemies, and forgive one another, over and over. And, if we do proclaim these things, you can bet we'll look like fools to many.

Jesus told some strange, laughable stories, like the one about somebody giving a big, fancy dinner; and nobody could come, or they thought they had better things to do. And the host ended up filling his big, fancy house with the muddy shoes of a rag-tag bunch of yahoos and ne'er do wells, most of whom didn't have a pot to spit in. Or the one Jesus told about the laborers who worked all day and got the same pay as those who came at the end of the day. You've got to be kidding. Or the one about the kid who gets his old man to fork over what he'd been saving for the kid's future and the kid goes off and spends it all up and comes home, because he had nobody else who'd take him in, and the father welcomes him home with open arms and no conditions. Foolishness.

The Apostle Paul boasted of his weakness, of all things. He preached a Christ crucified for people who didn't much care one way or the other, a savior who hung out with losers and died for sinners. It didn't make much sense to a lot of folks Paul tried to explain it to then, or to many folks now either. Maybe it's something you really can't explain very well, but can only live it- at least at times, by what you perceive is the grace of God.

Archbishop Desmond Tutu of South Africa, who for so long had no citizenship in his own country, talked about Jesus' parable of the Lost Sheep. He said most of us have distorted that parable. (We try to make them sound more reasonable to us.) He said: "...if you look at our religious pictures, most always Jesus is shown as the good shepherd carrying a nice fluffy, frisky lamb. Now frisky lambs are not known to stray away from their mommies. The sheep that is likely to stray is the recalcitrant old ram. And that is the one the good shepherd is prepared to leave ninety-nine perfectly behaved sheep to go after. And when he finds it, it has probably been through a wire fence which tore its fleece, and it has fallen into a dirty ditch of water. That smelly, ugly, unattractive one is the sheep that the good shepherd takes on his shoulders, brings back home rejoicing and says, 'Let's have a gig- I found the one that was lost.'" [31]

That raises a lot of questions for me, not only about those society has often viewed as worthless, that we've given up on, avoided, even removed from our midst; but also, about how we view ourselves, and what the grace of God has done or can do in retrieving us. Because it seems to me that before we can begin to understand any of it, we must know ourselves in some way as that lost sheep, that recalcitrant old ram, that prodigal child. Now, I don't have all the answers about all of that. I'm not sure the Archbishop does either. But, maybe it says something about why Tutu waded out into an angry mob, risking his life to save somebody who was a traitor in Tutu's own country. And, it might say something about why, after speaking at Columbia Seminary, (and I was there) when reporters from all over the world were anxiously waiting to ask him about all

---

[31] Desmond Tutu, "Grace Upon Grace," *Journal for Preachers*, Advent 1991, p. 22.

the important political questions of the day, he was out on the back steps of the Columbia Presbyterian Church, playing with children.

As I've thought about some of those things, I've thought also about Dr. Sam Hay. After he left this church, he became pastor of the First Presbyterian Church of Auburn, Alabama, a university town. It was in the 1940s, some of you might remember. He was a person with a lot of gifts, no doubt a lot of opportunities. And I wonder how many folks told him he'd be crazy to leave there, and to be the President of Stillman College, a little black school in Tuscaloosa, AL. I wonder how many people told him he'd be wasting his potential, wasting his life. It must have looked foolish to some. But Paul said: "God chose what is low and despised in the world…"

Maybe it's because I'm coming to another milestone in my life, another time when I'm thinking about my own call, that this passage has spoken so deeply to me again. But then, it's not just a word for me, and for you only to overhear. It's not just a word for ordained clergy. When Paul said, "Consider your call…." he was saying it to all those who had been called to follow Christ. "Consider your call…not many of you were wise according to worldly standards." I can vouch for that. "Not many of you were powerful, not many of you were of noble birth…" But we have been called to use the gifts we've been given, to use the everyday situations of our lives, to take the opportunities that arise, to risk looking like fools to be faithful; to trust that God can and will work beyond our understanding,

I remember seeing a television program that caught my attention. There was a woman in Raleigh, NC who, three times a week, would walk through the halls of the Wake Forest Medical Center in a white flowing dress, wheeling a harp like some angel of mercy, or some fool escaped from the top floor. She said she'd asked God how to do something for a hurting world. She wanted to give something back for the love she felt in her own life. And so, she began to go to the hospital, to the NICU, the ICU for premature babies. She said she went at first to play for the nurses, to do something for those giving the real help, working long hours under tense pressures. But after a while, what the medical personnel began to discover was that the music – or this woman's presence, or both- for some unexplained reason, helped slow the heart rate of the babies, to soothe them, to help them grow stronger.

There are times I feel like I can't help anybody; times I wonder what in the world I'm doing; times I feel like what I'm doing is pure foolishness. And sometimes I'm sure it is. But, to judge by the world's standards, as we all do sometimes, might well be to lose sight of our calling, and who it is who's called us, the One who's power is made perfect in our weakness. For the foolishness of God is wiser than human beings, and the weakness of God is stronger than human beings. Remember your call.

Blessed

Genesis 1-2:3

I don't know how often you have turned to the first couple of chapters of Genesis, the stories of creation that are there, but it really is magnificent language, some of the most magnificent language in all of scripture. It is about the One who created the world out of nothing but God's love, the God who also loved this world so much as to take on flesh and blood and become incarnate in Jesus Christ. Now there are a lot of religions that seek to escape this world, but our faith calls us to love it more deeply. In this world we will find God and God will find us.

I remember one of my family's pastors telling about a man who was a member of one of his congregations. He said that the man at times would come in late to worship, sometimes come in very late to worship, so that you would wonder why in the world he even bothered to come at all by then. The pastor thought about it, wondered about it, and finally at some point asked the man about it. The man said, "I try to come to worship whenever I can, but sometimes work and other commitments cause me to be late. Still, the one thing, *the one thing*, that I don't want to miss is the Benediction. Not because it signals the end of worship, but because I don't want to miss the blessing." He said, "I need the blessing, every week."

"Benediction" means a spoken blessing. In our tradition it's not so much a prayer as it is a pronouncement, a gift to us as we take it into the world. Now I don't know, at least as far as I can remember, I don't know why I've never preached specifically on blessings. I mean I've talked about a lot of blessings, but never, that I remember, focused directly on "blessing" itself. And yet there is so much of it in scripture, so basic to the faith that we profess from the first words in Genesis to some of the very last words in Revelation.

When the expectant mother, Mary, comes to her cousin Elizabeth's house, Elizabeth blesses her. She says Mary is "blessed of women." And old Simeon, when he sees the child, blesses him and his parents, Mary and Joseph, and he offers his well-remembered benediction: "Now let thy servant depart in peace, for mine eyes have seen thy salvation." The crowd shouts blessings to Jesus as he comes into Jerusalem on that Palm Sunday: "Blessed is the one that comes in the name of the Lord." And Jesus blesses his disciples as he ascends into heaven.

Many of us speak of blessings all the time. You know you can hardly sneeze, at least in these parts, without someone saying: "Bless you." A favorite expression around here is, of course, "Bless your heart," said one way or another. Many of us speak of them. You see car tags with "I'm blessed" written on them. People will tell you, "Count your blessings," as if you could. Thousands of people crowd into St. Peter's square to get a blessing from the Pope. We call what we say over meals, a blessing, even if it's not offered by a paid preacher.

My first prayer, at least the first one I remember, that I would say at night in my bed was: "Jesus tender shepherd, bless your little lamb tonight. Be here near me in the night. Keep me safe 'til morning light." And then I would say, "God bless Mommy, God bless Daddy, God bless my sisters." You know, asking for God's blessing on us and those we love, I suspect makes up a major part of what most of us say as prayers. The President and many politicians end speeches with, "God bless the United States of America," and others add on their bumper stickers, "God bless the people of all nations." Which reveals that sometimes we want to bless each other out.

There are special gatherings: to bless the troops, to bless the ships, to bless shrimp boats on the coast, and to bless crops in the fields of South Georgia, and even those to bless animals. There is a Presbyterian church in the Atlanta area that makes a regular ritual out of blessing the animals. And people will come with their pets but sometimes won't come with their neighbors.

I've been asked to offer blessings for all kinds of things: ball teams, civic club meetings, the state legislature - I wasn't sure how that one worked. I've blessed hospitals; I've blessed food pantries; I've blessed college facilities; I've done all kinds of things with blessings I wouldn't mention here. When some of us worked with Habitat for Humanity and a house was finished, we would gather in the living room with the people, and we would hold hands and bless the home. And we would bless the families, the people that were living there, which I think was probably the most important thing of all that we did.

When my children were teenagers and they would get in their cars, I would go out and stand in the driveway, and as they were pulling out with their friends I would be making the sign of the cross and they would take it to mean "Buckle your seat belt." Which it did! It was meant to remind them to buckle their seat belts, but it was also a sign of the cross, a blessing for them on their way and an appeal to God to bless them, to protect them, and to keep them safe. "Child of Blessing, child of Promise," we sing at baptisms of our children oftentimes. "Baptized with the Spirit's sign, with this water God has sealed you unto love and grace divine." The words are so beautiful that every time we sing them during those baptisms my eyes get misty. They're so powerful. We claim and pronounce God's blessing as we sing them. We know that we can't always protect them. We know that they won't always follow our best advice. So, we give them up, trusting them to the one to whom they truly belong. Even God's blessing won't protect them from all harm, physical, mental, emotional. But there is in this blessing at baptism, the promise that whatever comes… whatever comes, nothing can separate them from the love of God. God is their keeper, and ours.

People will scheme for blessings. People will fight to gain the favor of someone. And often they'll get it. And they'll get it, sometimes, in unexpected ways – blessings in disguise we might say. The scriptures talk about how Jacob beat his brother Esau out of a blessing, deceiving his old blind father, Isaac. You remember the story. And he went on to live in great prosperity – he got what he wanted.

Years later Jacob had a dream where he wrestled with a stranger in the night, and they wrestled all night long until the dawn. And Jacob thought at that point that he had the upper hand, as he always seemed to have, until, just at that moment, the stranger reached out and touched his thigh and put his hip out of joint. It's like Jacob had given all he had and then the stranger had shown him just how powerless he really was. But still, Jacob held on with a death grip, saying that he would not release the stranger until the stranger blessed him.

As Frederick Buechner tells it, what Jacob sees there in the dawn's first light is something more terrible than the face of death – it is the face of love. He says it's "vast and strong, half ruined with suffering, fierce with joy." [32] What Jacob gets is not a blessing that he can have now, by the strength of his cunning, or the force of his will, but a blessing he can have only as a gift. It comes only as a gift. He walked off wounded, with a limp the rest of his life, blessed.

---

[32] Frederick Buechner, *The Magnificent Defeat*, The Seabury Press, New York, 1979, p.18.

Despite what we often think, being blessed doesn't always have to do with wealth or popularity, or what we often call success or even health. I've heard some very poor people and some very sick people say, "I'm blessed. I am truly blessed!" Jesus in his Sermon on the Mount, the part we know as the Beatitudes, says blessed are the poor. Blessed are those who mourn. Blessed are you when you are reviled and persecuted for righteousness sake. Blessed are those who know they are loved, who know they belong to God, whatever comes. Some of us don't know that, not really. God pursues us all, not only to give us blessings or so that we will more clearly see the blessings that we have been given, but also so that we will be blessings to others. Like what the children sang about this morning.

Abraham and Sarah were told that through them all the nations of the world would be blessed. Preacher, teacher and author, Barbara Brown Taylor, says that pronouncing a blessing puts us as close to God as you can get. In Webster's Dictionary I found that to bless is "to infuse holiness into someone or something." But she says that God's creations are already infused with holiness. It is our calling to recognize that and maybe to help a person or thing to recognize it too.[33] We are told in Genesis that God made the world, the whole world, and it was good. Very Good! The moon and the stars, the mountains and rivers, the oceans and deserts, plants and animals, big ones, little ones, cuddly ones, creepy ones, - God blesses them all.

I stood on a mountain path recently watching my grandson hold a tiny red salamander, with great reverence. I had almost stepped on it, not noticing as I hurried along. Blessing means we stop and notice and give thanks to God. In blessing God's world, we are blessed. As God's children we're called to help fill up the holes in people's lives; to help them see themselves more as the people that they were

---

[33] Barbara Brown Taylor, *An Altar in the World: A Geography of Faith*, Harper One, New York, 2009, pp. 203-206.

created to be, as capable and worthy, as loving and lovable. We are even to bless those who curse us, the Apostle said. Our words have great power. They cannot be taken back. In all the things that we say to one another, and all the things we wear on our shirts, or put on our bumpers, the world needs to hear more blessing. In recognizing our blessings and being blessings to others we are then able to bless God.

The Psalms are full of blessings for God. "Bless the Lord, O my soul, and all that is within me bless God's holy name" (Psalms 103:1). You see it is not done easily or lightly. But we can all do it. We are all called to do it. It's not just something for priests or preachers to do. We do it by the power that works within us, that's able to do far more than we could ever ask or think (Ephesians. 3:20).

God bless you all, in in the name of the Father, the Son, and the Holy Spirit. Amen

In All My Remembering
Philippians 1:1-11

It's been a while since I've seen the pews filled with so many... happy people. I have been grateful, particularly over these last weeks, for so many letters and cards, e-mails and texts, phone calls and visits and the community reception. It has been hard to get much done that I thought I needed to get done. My friend, former colleague and mentor, Ike Kennerly, told me not to believe everything they tell you when you're leaving. But the truth is, though I don't believe it all, I'm still grateful for your expressions of love and care that you have given to me- to us all- through the years. I originally was told that I would have the last word today. But now I'm told there will be some brief time later for rebuttal. I did ask for you to be fed first. I hoped that would help things go better.

The text this morning comes from Paul's Letter to the Church in Philippi. I would tend to think that many preachers have turned to this text on similar occasions. But I don't really know since I've usually been busy myself at those times. The Letter to the Philippians has been called the "Epistle of Joy." Paul's letters often reveal strained relationships. Shoot, he got kicked out of several places. But, apparently his relationship with the Philippians was especially joyful. He speaks of their love and calls them to keep growing in the love of God and reaching out in love to others. That seemed fitting to me.

I saw a cartoon in which a minister is seated across from someone who's trying to help him find a call. The minister says: "I feel called to pastor wealthy little county-seat churches where they all love one another and adore preachers." [34] Sounds good to me. From time to

---

[34] *Pulpit Help*, 1999.

time people have asked me how I discerned a call to ministry. I'm reminded of Frederick Buechner telling of a woman who asked him about his call. She said: "Was it your own idea or were you poorly advised?"[35]

I can't tell you the exact moment. I was raised by parents who not only attended regularly but were heavily involved in Presbyterian churches. My mother had reformed a Methodist. He became a Presbyterian elder, taught Sunday School and spoke at church suppers. As in the words of my oldest child once when he was asked what he'd been up to, and he said: "Go to church, go to church, go to church", so it was for us.

There were several Presbyterian ministers in my mother's family. Church, theology and how we were to live out our faith were regular topics of conversation. I am a product of Christian nurture. Not that that always must lead to becoming an ordained minister. I believe we are all called by God to various kinds of ministry not only in the church but in our daily work and careers. As Paul says, we are partners in ministry.

I went to Presbyterian College as did several of my extended family members. I was majoring in English and thought I might become a news reporter like some I'd known in my church and neighborhood growing up. I took Religion courses because they were required at PC and I was better at them than at Biology and Math. Then, like some others through the years, I was invited to come out to fill the pulpits of small congregations in the countryside. I was 18 when I first went. I then started preaching regularly at the Lickville Presbyterian Church with my friend Ted Wardlaw. I shudder to think what those poor people endured from sermons finished as we

---

[35] Frederick Buechner, *Listening to Your Life*, Harper, San Francisco, 1992, p.227.

pulled into the church parking lot on Sunday mornings. But they kept asking us back and laying out dinner for us afterwards at their farm houses and teaching us the love of God. They called me "pastor."

I went on to Columbia Theological Seminary where my former pastor at Decatur Presbyterian Church was the president and took courses from professors I'd known through my church. For Presbyterians, you aren't allowed to just go and start a church when you feel called. You not only have to go through seminary, but you must take a battery of personality and psychological tests like the Minnesota Multiphasic Personality Inventory. I wondered if Jesus would pass with all that stuff about thinking, he was human and divine. Then, somebody else must believe you're called to ministry in some fashion with them. And the Presbytery (other Presbyterians in your area) must agree. Fortunately, the Westminster Presbyterian Church in Charleston, SC did issue me a call to be the Associate Pastor there in 1980. As for the First Presbyterian Church of Covington, it was pretty much a wealthy little county–seat church.

I've been asked if I believe God gives us signs at times. My grandmother, a preacher's daughter and wife of a Presbyterian College Bible teacher, used to say that some of the students at PC claimed they had seen a "GP" in the sky, and took it as a sign to Go Preach. But she thought that for many of them it had meant, Go Plow.

I have to say I do believe in signs. I believe they are in the eyes of the beholder, or the ears. Once when Jesus was praying, some around him heard an angel speaking to him, but others only thought it had thundered. I remember preaching on signs at one point and telling about a water stain (no longer there) on the ceiling of the men's restroom that looked to me exactly like George Washington. Don't ask. After worship, several people crowded in to see it. My mother was here, and she went with the crowd. I'm not sure how far she got in, but she said to me: "Sugar, I just didn't see it." I said: "Mama, it's all in the angle from which you look at it." Signs.

For me, my call to Westminster had been confirmed when I got off the plane for the interview. I was dressed in my new black suit which I'd just discovered had smears all over the coat lapel, from where my toddler had wiped his mouth. But as I looked down at Ike's shoes when he greeted me; there was a blob of baby food, and I began to think maybe this will work.

My call here started with hearing a voice, just as I had returned from a visit to another church. I'd already made a couple of visits there, and this last one really had been to make some final arrangements. I literally had just told Theodosia I believed it was the place we were to go, when the phone rang. The voice said, "Billy, this is Steve Jordan from Covington, Georgia. You probably have heard we've lost our minister." I said, yes, I had heard that since I was presently working with that minister, Bob Dunham. We laughed. He said, "I know you might already be headed somewhere else, but we'd like to talk with you if you haven't made a final decision." And you know, in that conversation, it felt like I was about to walk down the aisle and was having thoughts about another woman. I went to Covington to see.

The committee consisted of Steve, Bill Moncrief, Dean of Oxford College, Donald Stephenson, Fran Prince, a teenager named Michelle Tingler (now Green) and Louly Hay. Louly says she and Fran were determined to hold out against the men who seemed to already have their minds made up. They were a harder sell. I have outlasted them all here, but Louly, who moderated my official ouster last Sunday. She, next to God as the Psalmist says, has been my keeper in all my going out and coming in.

A small church in a small town seemed just right. As I was mulling it over, I said something to my friend, Don Frampton, a minister and child of a minister, that I would be getting less as the pastor of the new church than as the associate pastor of the old one. He said: "Don't worry, they'll make it up in cukes and maters" (produce). The truth has been that we have received more in many ways than we ever would have imagined.

Paul says, we have a partnership in the Gospel. We believe in the priesthood of all believers. You have pastored me and my family. We have been supported, encouraged, fretted over and prayed over. Members of this congregation have stood by us in our sickness and in our sorrow, spoken words of hope and been examples of faith when we've needed them most. I am continually amazed at the commitment and dedication of many who have given long hours of service to the church beyond the demands of your own jobs and family responsibilities and have ministered to others in some situations more effectively than I ever could. We have been greatly blessed.

I remember one of my first Sundays leading worship here, in the old sanctuary. Our littlest one, Grady, was standing at the vent in the bottom of the door to the nursery down the hall. And I (and others) could hear his crying. C. T. Bohannan got up from his pew, went down the hall and picked him up and walked him around. So many others have picked up my children, and Theodosia and me, in many ways just as we promise one another at baptism. I felt called to a place where I would know everybody and be able to share their lives, where maybe I could speak the language. It has been a special privilege to do so through generations, doing weddings for children of people I married, baptizing the children of some I baptized, ordaining as elders some I taught in confirmation classes.

Living in a small community is like living in a fish bowl. But it has been to me like having a parish ministry. People from other churches sometimes show up here for a second opinion. Some here go other places at times for the same reason.

As I was walking down the street not long ago, a local lawyer stopped his car and yelled out the window at me: "It's good to see a preacher with his hands in his own pockets for a change." A lawyer! Here you know people on the School Board, the City Council and Board of Commissioners, judges, police officers. People gather for coffee regularly and offer you a place at the table at lunch when you come in by yourself. We visit one another in the hospital and gather in the cemetery for funerals.

I remember celebrating Ed Robinson's 80th birthday. He and Betty Belairs (just a bit younger than Ed, she reminded me) had said years before, if they got that far, they'd ride motorcycles around the square on their birthdays. Fortunately, it had rained some that day and they were convinced not to do that. But people still filled People's Drug Store and flowed out into the street. So, we put chairs in the back of my son Cam's truck and drove them around the square as a host of people cheered on the sidewalks. About midway around the square, I noticed blue lights flashing. I thought, oh no, no parade license. As I pulled back into the space at People's, the officers got out and came up to me. One said: "Mayor Ramsey sent us as an escort."

In this church, through the years, we've sought to make connections with the community across many lines that separate us. We've had pulpit swaps, community services at Holy Week and Thanksgiving, Taizé services. We've done Bible School and mission together, sung in an Ambassador Choir- ambassadors of reconciliation across the lines of race and religion. And over the years we have welcomed here an increasing diversity into this congregation that has changed our conversation among ourselves. We don't claim to have the whole truth here. We are part of a larger body that communes around a table that stretches far beyond this little one here. We don't believe ultimately in Presbyterianism, or even Christianity, but in the Christ, who loves us all and stretches us toward loving others.

I am thankful for your partnership in ministry from the first day until now as Paul said. The faith to which Christ calls us is not just a matter between him and me or him and you. It involves "us." We are called into a community of faith. Jesus said, "Where two or more are gathered in my name, there I am in the midst of you." We are part of a body – Christ's body- diverse and multi-talented. Only by God's grace and only together are we saints. Claimed by God in baptism, we learn a language foreign and foolish to many, the language of confession and forgiveness, redemption and resurrection; we are fed the bread of life and offered the cup of salvation and are sent out into the world every week with God's power and blessing.

Somebody came in to see me this week to say good-bye. He said he wouldn't be here today. After talking a while, he said, "Thanks for the sermons." He said, "I don't think I agree with all of them." I said, "Good!" When I was installed here, Steve Jordan, in his remarks about being a shepherd and pastor and all that, said: "But don't let us always be comfortable. We need you to challenge us, to keep us searching and probing for what God intends for our lives." God's not always easy to listen to. Every sermon I preach, I preach to me first. Oh, there are some folks I think about, but they never seem to be here when I think they need to hear something. And there have been so many times when I've thought: Jesus said what? You've got to be kidding! Who's going to believe that?

I'm grateful for other preachers who've preached here regularly through the years. Because sometimes preachers begin to think theirs is the only voice of God. And worse, sometimes the congregation begins to believe that. From time to time when things have been difficult, I've gone out in the hallway and had some serious conversations with those pastors whose pictures are hanging out there. And sometimes, I've looked up on the wall to make sure my picture wasn't hanging up there with the former pastors. And if not, I've gone on back to my study to try again. I know Moses pleaded with God for God to give him some other people to help him do the work and make decisions, and then later pleaded with God to do away with them because they were making decisions Moses didn't like. I understand that.

But, I've looked out every week on people who have many gifts I don't have. This congregation is so blessed with singers, and musicians. Sometimes at Christmas Eve we've had to cut back on people participating in worship because it looked too much like *America's Got Talent*. We have artists and writers, gardeners and crafts people, builders and cooks, doctors and lawyers, city council members, a mayor, a state senator, an inventor of the FAX machine and a Pulitzer Prize winner. We have people passionate for mission; people who've started and led so many good things in this community. We have people from seven or eight different countries in this little congregation. God has done so much through us. Oh, change isn't easy. We grow comfortable with many things as they have been.

Your next pastor will have gifts I don't have. Nobody has them all. But that person will be surrounded by people who have many gifts that God is calling you to use in Christ's name. The greatest of which is love. We are part of a long line of witnesses. This church has been in the middle of this town for 162 years. It has survived its sanctuary burning to the ground and having a hole blown in its roof by lightening. It has survived being dissolved and struggling to start all over again. It has thrived because God keeps doing new things. This is God's church.

Like Paul, I give thanks to God for your partnership in ministry from my first day until now. I hold you in my heart. I thank God in all (or most) of my remembrance of you, keeping you in my prayers, praying that your love may abound more and more. And I am sure that the One who began a good work in you will bring it to completion at the day of Jesus Christ. Bless you all in His name.

www.ingramcontent.com/pod-product-compliance
Lightning Source LLC
Chambersburg PA
CBHW052138110526
44591CB00012B/1778